AGES 5-7

SCHOLASTIC

Sight Words
Jumbo Workbook

This book belongs to

_____

Editor: Tara Welty
Cover design by Tannaz Fassihi
Cover art by Gabriele Antonini
Interior design by Radames Espinoza
Interior illustrations by Maxie Chambliss, Jane Dippold, Rusty Fletcher, Lucia Kemp Henry,
Doug Jones, Mike Moran, The Noun Project, and Danny E. Rivera
Stock Images @ Shutterstock.com

ISBN 978-1-338-73934-3

4 5 6 7 8 9 10   144   21 22 23 24 25 26 27 28

Dear Family,

Research shows that 50 percent of everything we read is made up of just 100 "sight words"—those common, unglamorous, hard-to-decode words such as *the, of, is, your,* and *there.*

Teachers have long agreed that a mastery of sight words is the golden key to unlocking reading confidence. But how do busy children find the time to commit all of these tricky words to memory?

Welcome to the *Sight Words Jumbo Workbook*! This lively resource is the perfect tool to target and teach the top 100 sight words in just minutes a day. That's because the pages that follow are fun, engaging, and designed to motivate even the most reluctant learners. And here's more good news: Most of the easy-to-do activities can be completed by children *all by themselves...* and likely with a smile!

So why not begin today? Just turn the page and start your child on the path to a lifetime of reading success.

Happy learning,

The Editors

About This Book

This *Sight Words Jumbo Workbook* is here to help your child master the top 100 sight words. (For a list of those words, see page 10.) The book is designed to focus on four sight words at a time, running through a sequence of kid-pleasing activities to ensure the learning sticks. The pages are varied and playful. Here are some examples:

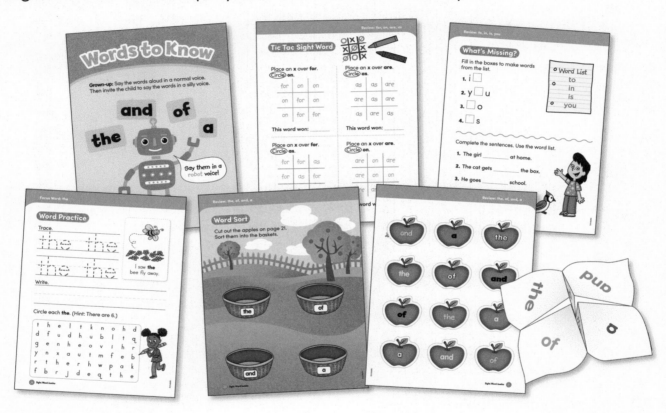

The goal of this workbook is to teach sight words. But, along the way, children will have a chance to boost other essential skills including:

- Following Directions
- Speaking
- Reading
- Writing
- Coloring

- Sorting
- Cutting*
- Pasting
- Fine Motor
- Critical Thinking

* Always supervise children when working with scissors.

Scholastic Inc.

Extra, Extra!

But wait, there's more! These special components are guaranteed to make learning extra fun...

SIGHT WORD BOOSTERS

In addition to what you'll find on the workbook pages, we've provided no-prep activities you and your child can do together to cement sight word learning. (See page 11.)

INSTANT FLASH CARDS

Snip out the flash cards for all 100 sight words on pages 307–318. We've also provided ideas for using the cards for instant games, as well as an informal assessment to ensure your child has mastered every important word.

ONLINE LEARNING GAMES

Take learning online with fun learning games: **www.scholastic.com/success**

MOTIVATING STICKERS

What better way to mark the milestones of your child's learning than with colorful stickers? After a workbook session, they're the perfect way to say: "Job well done!"

REWARD CERTIFICATE

Last, but not least, celebrate your child's leaps in sight word fluency with this bright, pull-out certificate (page 320).

Table of Contents

Scholastic Inc.

Scholastic Inc.

Scholastic Inc.

Sight Word List

The *Sight Words Jumbo Workbook* targets and teaches 100 must-know words from the Fry Sight Words list. This list, created by a literacy expert, tracks the top words that appear in print in order of frequency. We encourage you to use these words with the extra activities on pages 11 and 305.

1. the	26. or	51. will	76. number
2. of	27. one	52. up	77. no
3. and	28. had	53. other	78. way
4. a	29. by	54. about	79. could
5. to	30. words	55. out	80. people
6. in	31. but	56. many	81. my
7. is	32. not	57. then	82. than
8. you	33. what	58. them	83. first
9. that	34. all	59. these	84. water
10. it	35. were	60. so	85. been
11. he	36. we	61. some	86. called
12. was	37. when	62. her	87. who
13. for	38. your	63. would	88. am
14. on	39. can	64. make	89. its
15. are	40. said	65. like	90. now
16. as	41. there	66. him	91. find
17. with	42. use	67. into	92. long
18. his	43. an	68. time	93. down
19. they	44. each	69. has	94. day
20. I	45. which	70. look	95. did
21. at	46. she	71. two	96. get
22. be	47. do	72. more	97. come
23. this	48. how	73. write	98. made
24. have	49. their	74. go	99. may
25. from	50. if	75. see	100. part

Sight Word Boosters

Make use of these extra activities to support your child's sight word journey. We also encourage you to develop your own creative ideas.

1. **LOOK IN BOOKS:** Choose a secret sight word from a page in a picture book. Give your child clues to guess what it is, such as: *It begins with the letter* y. *It rhymes with* to. *It has three letters.* Continue giving clues until your child guesses the word (*you*). Repeat with different sight words.

2. **SUPERMARKET TALLY:** Give your child a crayon and a clipboard with a list of five—or more—sight words to find at the supermarket, such as *the, an, with, is, have.* As your child goes through the store with you, challenge him or her to make an X each time a sight word is spotted on a product or sign. Which word wins by being spotted the most?

3. **SIGHT WORD COLLAGE:** Choose a single sight word, such as *about*, and encourage your child to cut that word out of magazines—in a variety of sizes and styles. Then use the cuttings to create a colorful sight word collage to display with pride!

4. **DRAW A DOG:** Choose a secret sight word, such as *other.* Build a sentence around it, writing blanks for each letter. For example: *The dog chased the _ _ _ _ _ dog around the yard.* Next, challenge your child to guess letters in the word. If the letter is in the word, write it in the space. If not, add one feature to your dog drawing. Can your child solve the word before the dog's face is complete?

5. **FLASH CARD FUN:** On pages 307–318 you'll find a complete set of sight word flash cards. Use them with the games on page 305 to expand sight word knowledge.

Making Fun Flaps

Making Fun Flaps is easy. Just follow these simple directions.

1 Cut out the Fun Flap along the dashed lines, so you have a square shape.

2 Place the Fun Flap on a flat surface with the blank side facing up.

3 Fold back the four corners along the solid lines so they touch in the center of the square.

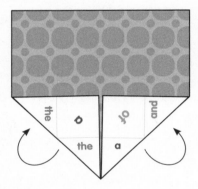

4 Turn over the Fun Flap. Fold back the corners again so that they touch the center of the square.

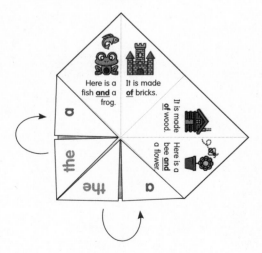

5 Fold the Fun Flap in half both ways.

6 Place your right thumb and index finger inside the two right flaps.

7 Place your left thumb and index finger inside the two left flaps.

8 Open and close the Fun Flap by moving your fingers.

9 Have fun!

HOW TO USE Hold the Fun Flap in the closed position, inviting your child to choose one of the four sight words and a number from 1 to 10. Open and close the Fun Flap that many times. Next, challenge your child to find that same sight word on an inside flap, open it up, and use the picture cue to read the sight word sentence. Repeat this activity several times, switching roles so your child has the opportunity to hold and manipulate the Fun Flap, too.

Words to Know

Grown-up: Say the words aloud in a normal voice. Then invite your child to say the words in a silly voice.

and

of

the

a

Say them in a robot voice!

Word Practice

Trace.

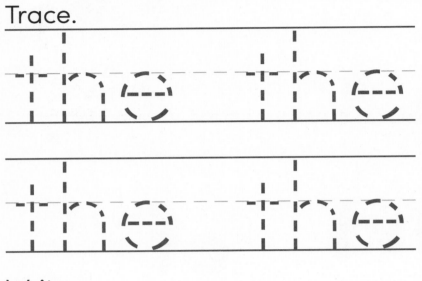

I saw **the** bee fly away.

Write.

Circle each **the**. (Hint: There are 6.)

t	h	e	l	t	k	n	o	h	d
d	f	u	d	h	u	b	l	t	q
g	e	n	h	e	o	v	i	h	r
y	n	x	a	u	t	m	f	e	b
r	r	t	h	e	r	h	w	p	a	k
f	b	r	j	d	e	q	t	h	e

Word Practice

Trace.

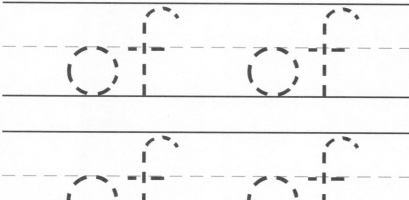

He has lots **of** blocks.

Write.

Find each **of**. Color that space yellow. Then color the rest of the picture.

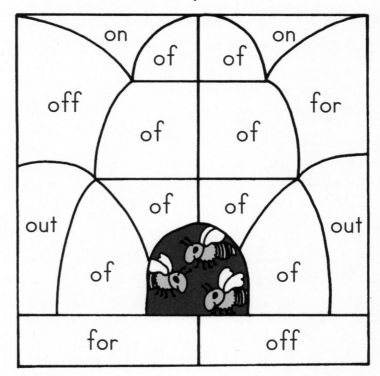

Word Practice

Trace.

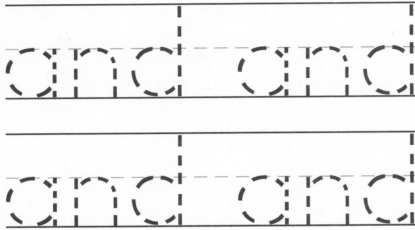

I have a bat
and a ball.

Write.

Help the dog get a treat! Color the rocks with **and**.

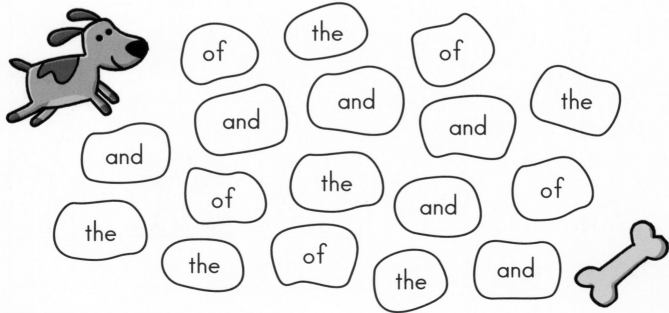

Scholastic Inc.

Word Practice

Trace.

This is **a** good book.

Write.

Circle each **a**. (Hint: There are 6.)

t a k f g r n s h o
q f u d c b r l m a
d o v h f a u i t p
f r x a n p m f c b
y l h e r t w a g k
a w z j d i q r s e

What's Missing?

Fill in the boxes to make words from the list.

1. a ☐ d

2. ☐ f

3. ☐

4. ☐ h e

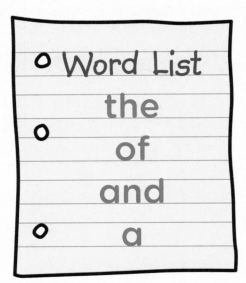

Word List
the
of
and
a

~~~~~~~~~~~~~~~~~~~~~~~~~~~~~

Complete the sentences. Use the word list.

1. Matt has _____ cat.

2. His cat is _____ orange one.

3. I like cookies _____ milk.

4. I want a slice _____ pizza.

Tic-Tac Sight Word

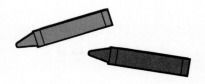

Play the games below. The word with three Xs or Os wins!

Place an **X** over **the**.
(Circle) **of**.

the	of	of
the	of	the
of	the	of

This word won: _____

Place an **X** over **and**.
(Circle) **a**.

and	a	a
and	a	and
a	and	and

This word won: _____

Place an **X** over **the**.
(Circle) **a**.

the	a	a
a	the	the
the	a	the

This word won: _____

Place an **X** over **and**.
(Circle) **of**.

and	of	of
and	and	of
of	of	and

This word won: _____

Scholastic Inc.

Word Sort

Cut out the apples on page 21.
Sort them into the baskets.

the

of

and

a

Scholastic Inc.

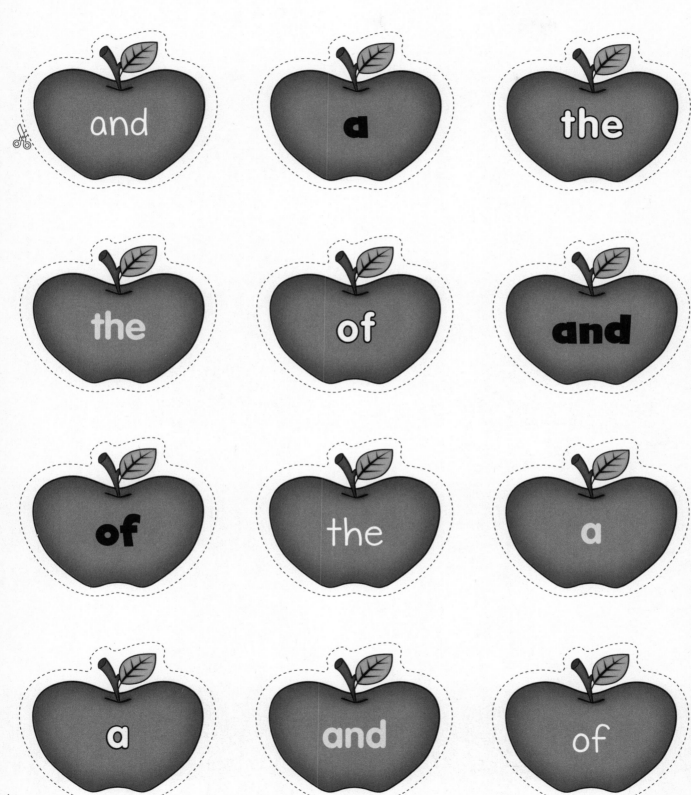

and

a

the

the

of

and

of

the

a

a

and

of

Sight Word Catcher

Cut and fold the Fun Flap.

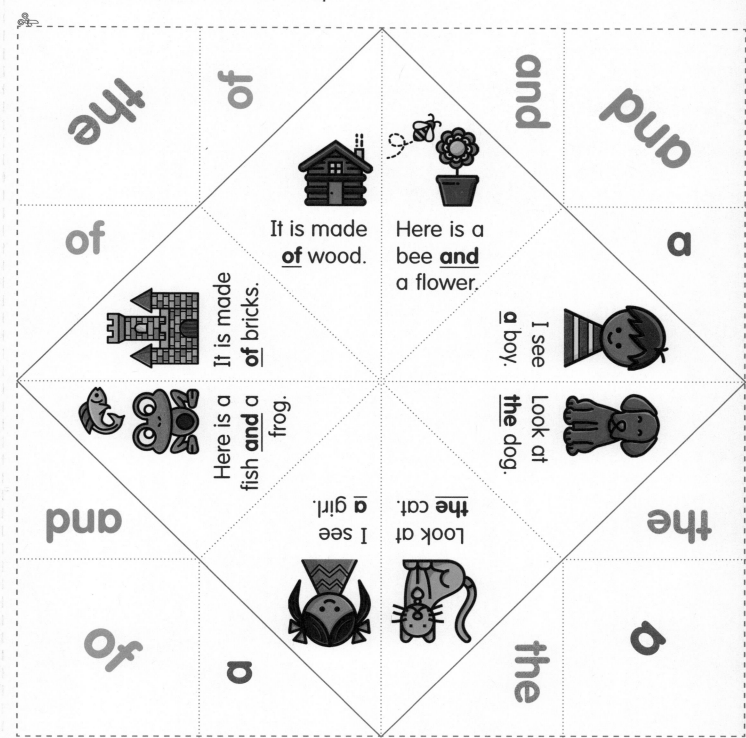

Words to Know

Grown-up: Say the words aloud in a normal voice. Then invite your child to say the words in a silly voice.

to is in you

Say them in a superhero voice!

Word Practice

Trace.

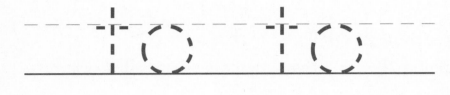

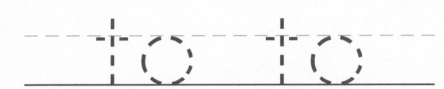

She wants **to** hold the rabbit.

Write.

Find each **to**.
Color that space **red**.
Then color the rest of the picture.

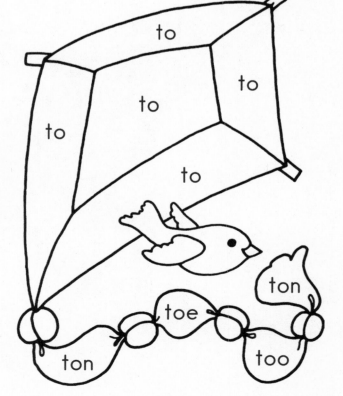

Scholastic Inc.

Word Practice

Trace.

We can go **in** the van.

Write.

Circle each **in**. (Hint: There are 6.)

y	l	h	i	n	t	i	j	m	k
p	f	u	d	c	q	n	w	g	a
d	i	v	b	f	n	r	i	n	z
c	n	x	e	o	g	v	p	h	b
e	a	r	y	i	n	k	l	i	f
m	u	z	s	d	t	q	j	n	o

Word Practice

Trace.

The baby **is** happy.

Write.

Find each **is**. Color that space **pink**.
Then color the rest of the picture.

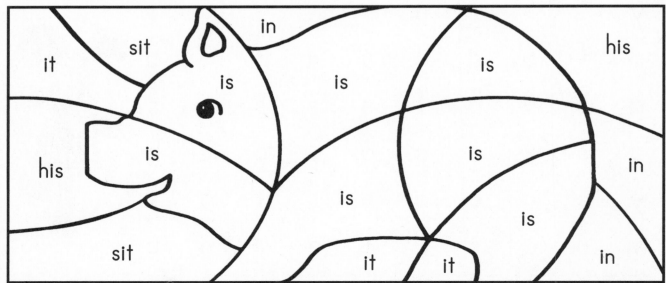

Scholastic Inc.

Word Practice

Trace.

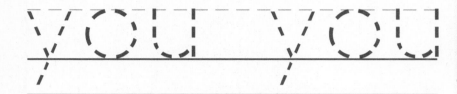

Do **you** have a cat?

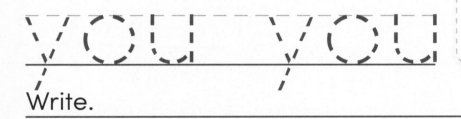

Write.

Circle each **you**. (Hint: There are 6.)

y	a	k	z	c	r	n	y	h	i
o	f	p	y	o	u	q	o	m	d
u	w	n	h	f	e	j	u	t	r
d	s	x	a	y	p	l	z	c	b
y	o	u	e	o	t	w	s	g	k
v	c	g	j	u	i	q	y	o	u

What's Missing?

Fill in the boxes to make words from the list.

1. ☐ s

2. y ☐ u

3. ☐ o

4. i ☐

Word List
to
in
is
you

Complete the sentences. Use the word list.

1. The girl _____ at home.

2. The cat gets _____ the box.

3. He goes _____ school.

4. Do _____ see the bird?

Sight Word Maze

Help Mama Rabbit find her baby rabbits.
Find the path with the word **you**.

Scholastic Inc.

Word Search

Circle the words from the word list. The words go across and down. The words appear more than once.

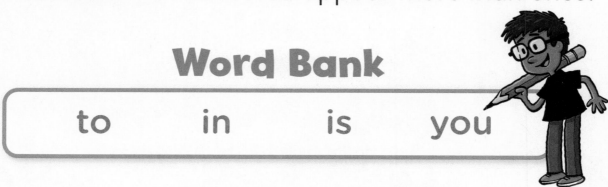

Word Bank

to	in	is	you

t m k z e s n y i s k z

o f p y o u q o m d p i

u w i h f e j u t r n n

d s n t o y o u o i x a

y i u e i s w d s s u e

t s g j u n i y e n o j

o x p y o u n o m d i n

u w y i s e j u t o n h

d z o x y p i n c b x i

i n u e s t o s e s u s

Sight Word Catcher

Cut and fold the Fun Flap.

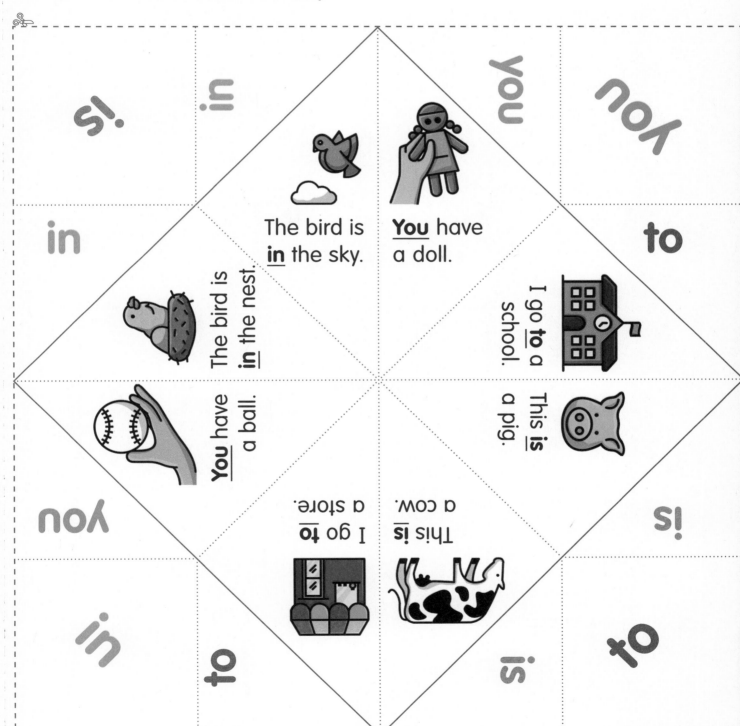

The bird is **in** the sky.

You have a doll.

The bird is **in** the nest.

You have a ball.

I go **to** a school.

This **is** a pig.

I go **to** a store.

This **is** a cow.

is

in

you

you

in

to

you

in

to

is

is

to

Words to Know

Grown-up: Say the words aloud in a normal voice. Then invite your child to say the words in a silly voice.

that he

it was

Say them in a **monster** voice!

Word Practice

Trace.

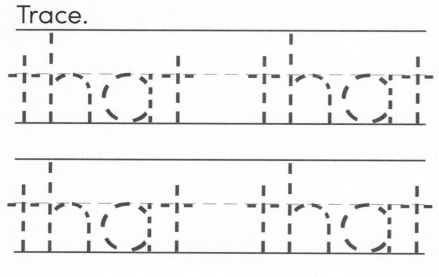

I want a pet
that swims.

Write.

Find each **that**. Color that ribbon **blue**.
Then color the rest of the picture.

that

hat

bat

then

that

that

that

the

Word Practice

Trace.

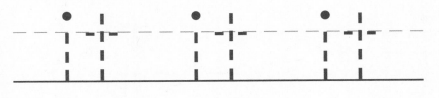

What time
is **it**?

Write.

Circle each **it**. (Hint: There are 6.)

h	x	i	t	e	r	s	j	k	i
z	f	w	d	i	b	u	l	y	t
k	p	n	h	t	o	z	i	t	v
i	t	g	x	y	n	p	m	f	c
y	l	h	o	c	i	w	a	g	b
f	a	v	j	d	t	q	e	s	r

Word Practice

Trace.

Where is **he** going?

Write.

Find each **he**. Color that space **green**. Then color the rest of the picture.

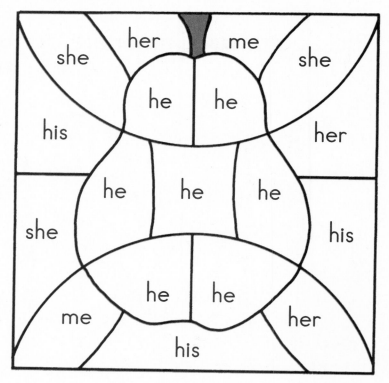

Word Practice

Trace.

The bird **was** in a tree.

Write.

Find each **was**. Color that cracker **orange**. Then color the rest of the picture.

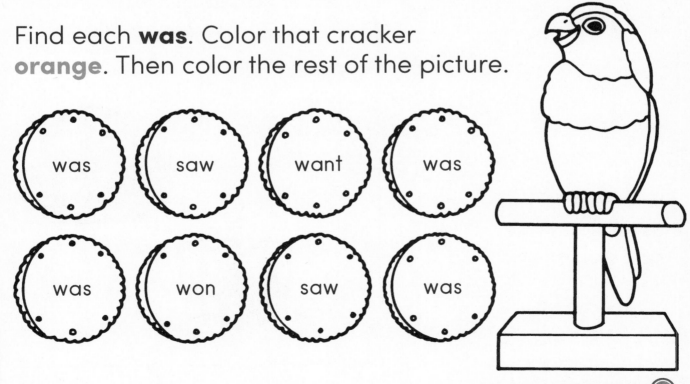

was   saw   want   was

was   won   saw   was

What's Missing?

Fill in the boxes to make words from the list.

1. ☐ e

2. w ☐ s

3. i ☐

4. t ☐ a t

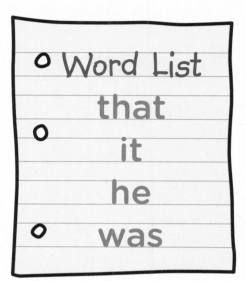

○ Word List
that
○ it
he
○ was

~~~~~~~~~~~~~~~~~~~~~~~~~~~~~~~

Complete the sentences. Use the word list.

1. Fred _____ at the park.

2. Will _____ eat the cake?

3. I will eat _____ .

4. I want _____ car.

Scholastic Inc.

Sight Word Color

Color the picture. Use the Color Key.

Color Key

that	Green
it	Blue
he	Red
was	Purple

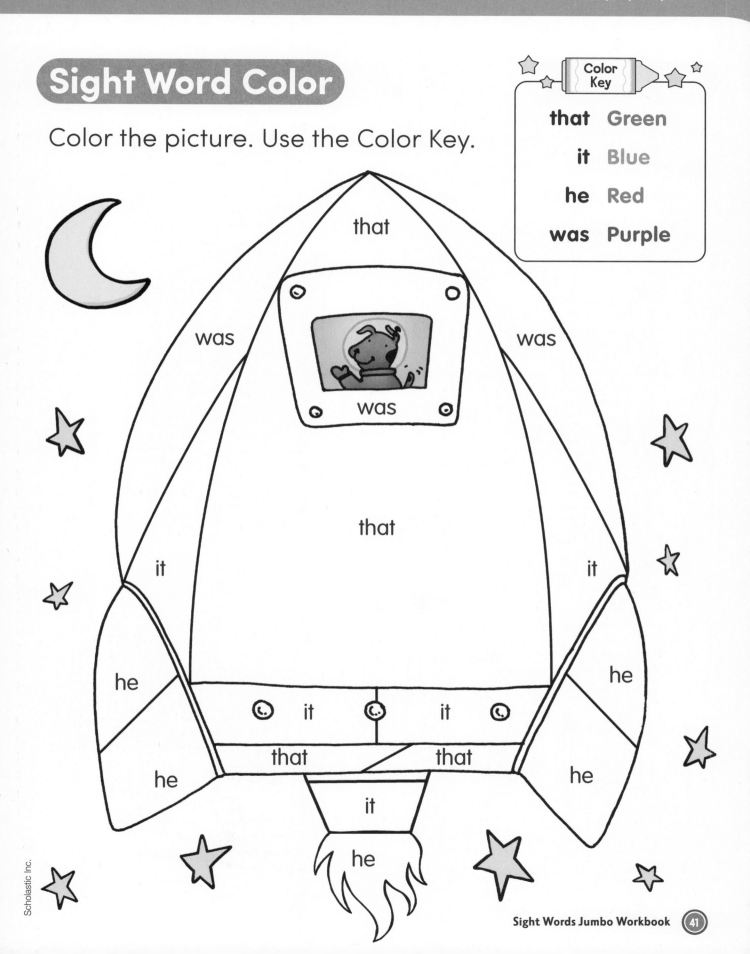

Word Sort

Cut out the spiders on page 43.
Sort them onto the webs.

Sight Word Catcher

Cut and fold the Fun Flap.

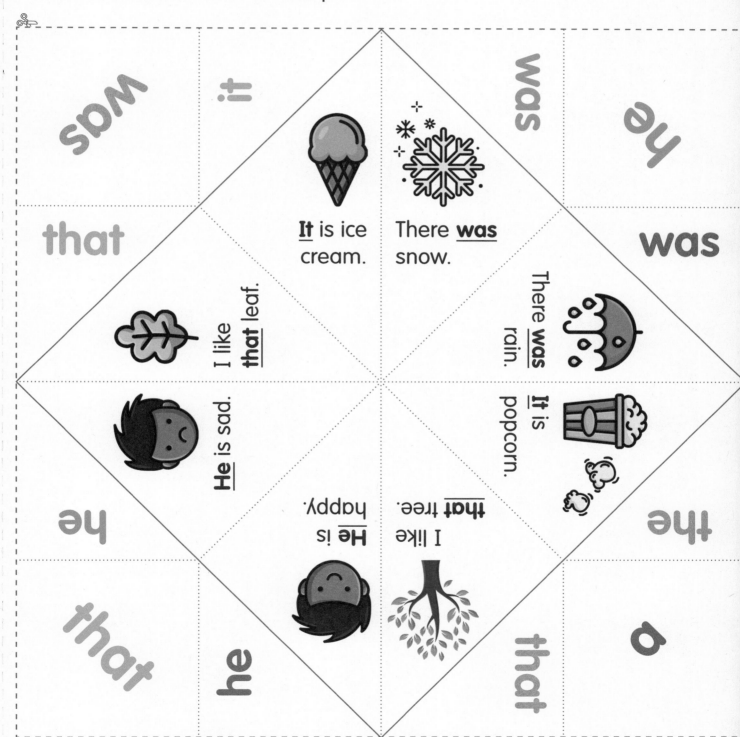

Words to Know

Grown-up: Say the words aloud in a normal voice. Then invite your child to say the words in a silly voice.

are

on

for

as

Say them in an underwater voice!

Word Practice

Trace.

for for for

for for for

This cake is **for** you.

Write.

Find each **for**. Color that space **red**.
Then color the rest of the picture.

Scholastic Inc.

Word Practice

Trace.

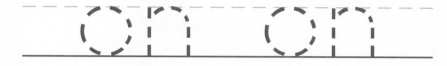

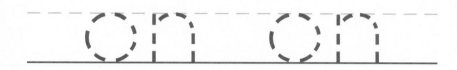

The bug is **on** a rock.

Write.

Find each **on**. Color that toy **blue**.
Then color the rest of the picture.

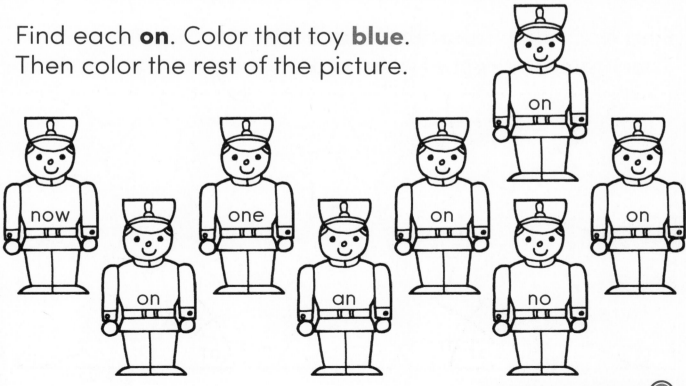

Word Practice

Trace.

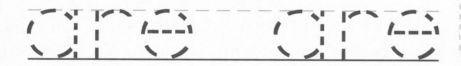

Hello, how **are** you?

Write.

Find each **are**. Color that star yellow.
Then color the rest of the picture.

air

am

are

arm

are

are

art

are

Word Practice

Trace.

Swing **as** high **as** you can.

Write.

Find each **as**. Color that space **green**.
Then color the rest of the picture.

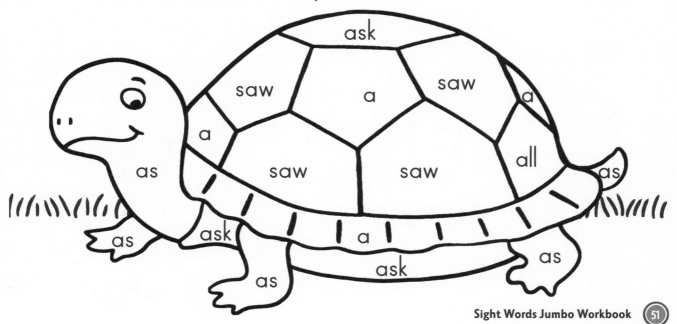

What's Missing?

Fill in the boxes to make words from the list.

1. a r ☐

2. ☐ n

3. f ☐ r

4. ☐ s

o **Word List**
for
o on
are
o as

Complete the sentences. Use the word list.

1. A hen is _____ the box.

2. This pie is _____ you.

3. I'm _____ fast as a horse.

4. We _____ at the post office.

Scholastic Inc.

Tic-Tac Sight Word

Play the games below. The word with three Xs or Os wins!

Place an **X** over **for**.
(Circle) **on**.

for	on	on
on	for	on
on	for	for

This word won: _____

Place an **X** over **are**.
(Circle) **as**.

as	as	are
are	are	are
as	are	as

This word won: _____

Place an **X** over **for**.
(Circle) **as**.

for	for	as
for	as	for
as	for	as

This word won: _____

Place an **X** over **are**.
(Circle) **on**.

are	on	are
on	on	on
are	are	on

This word won: _____

Word Sort

Cut out the penguins on page 55.
Sort them onto the ice floes.

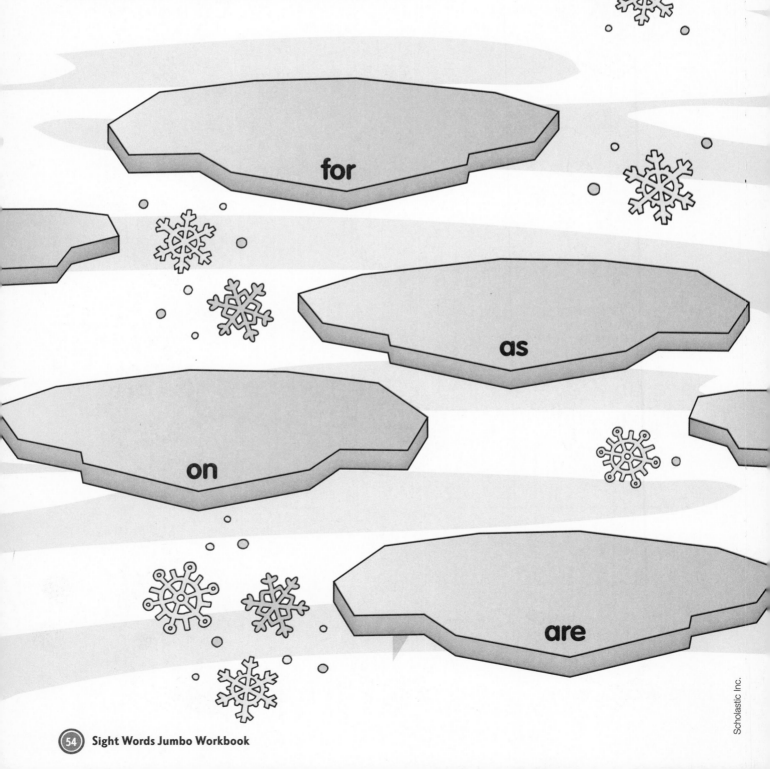

for

as

on

are

Sight Word Catcher

Cut and fold the Fun Flap.

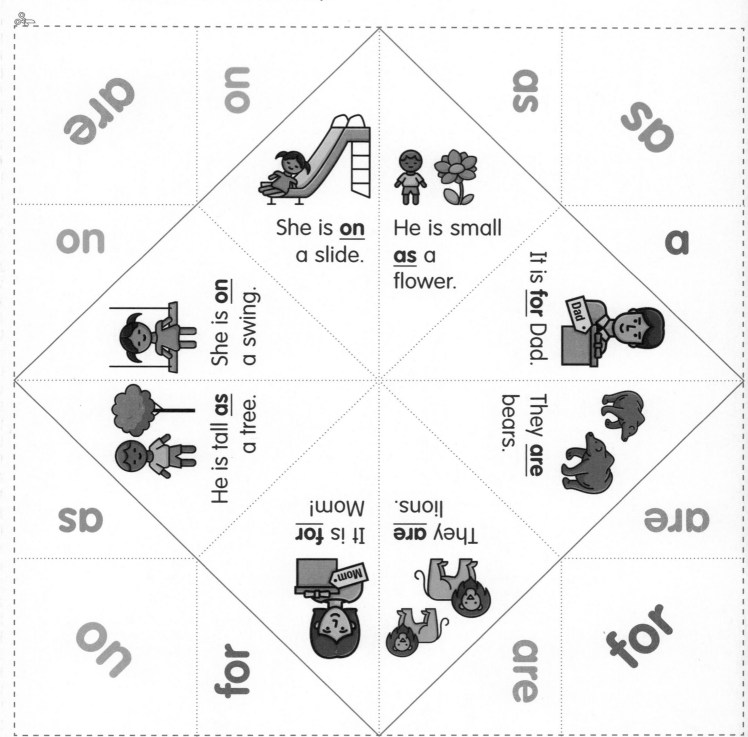

Words to Know

Grown-up: Say the words aloud in a normal voice. Then invite your child to say the words in a silly voice.

his

they

with

I

Say them in a parrot voice!

Word Practice

Trace.

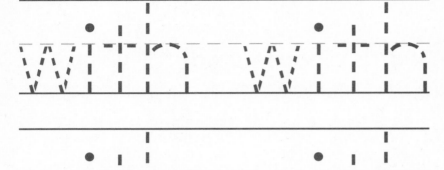

Come **with** me to the zoo.

Write.

Circle each **with**. (Hint: There are 6.)

p o w j a k w i t h h
w b i d u f r l m g
i e t m w i t h w n
t u h a n p v f i b
h l c e k o r s t y
d x q w i t h z h e

Word Practice

Trace.

his his

his his

The boy pats **his** dog.

Write.

Help the singer find the choir. Color the music notes with **his**.

Word Practice

Trace.

they they

they they

Will **they** take all the food?

Write.

Find each **they**. Color that space **orange**.
Then color the rest of the picture.

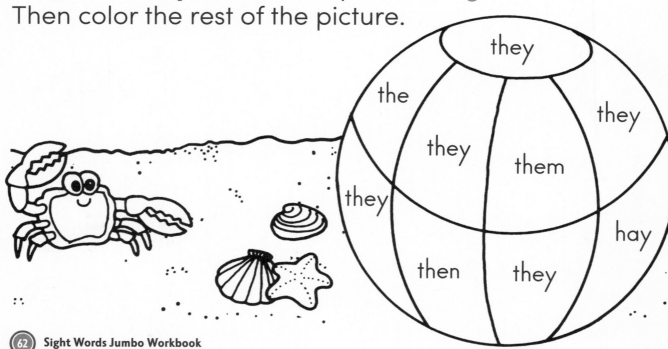

they

the

they

they

them

they

then

they

hay

Scholastic Inc.

Word Practice

Trace.

I I I I

I I I I

I like to ride the bus.

Write.

Circle each **I**. (Hint: There are 6.)

t a k f x w i t h I
h w i s I b u l m q
e i I s f z v y t h
y t h i s p I f c i
y h v e r h i s I s
f I r t h e y r s e

Scholastic Inc.

What's Missing?

Fill in the boxes to make words from the list.

o **Word List**
with
his
they
I

1. the ☐

2. ☐

3. h ☐ s

4. w i ☐ h

Complete the sentences. Use the word list.

1. _____ am cold.

2. The dog is _____.

3. Have dinner _____ Grandma.

4. Were _____ all at the park?

Scholastic Inc.

Sight Word Maze

Help the bird find its eggs. Connect a path by coloring each nest with a list word.

with	they
his	I

Start

can   your   will

I   with   they   his

you   about   each   I

she   how   they   with

out   I   his   can

there   with   if   will

many   they   his   End

Scholastic Inc.

Word Sort

Cut out the raindrops on page 67.
Sort them under the rain cloud.

they   I   his   with

Scholastic Inc.

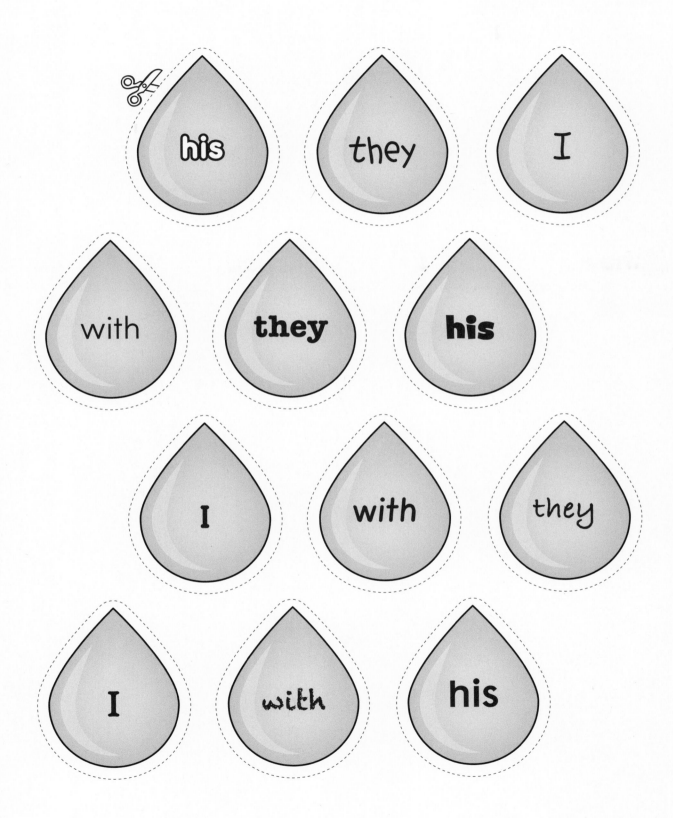

Sight Words Jumbo Workbook 67

Sight Word Catcher

Cut and fold the Fun Flap.

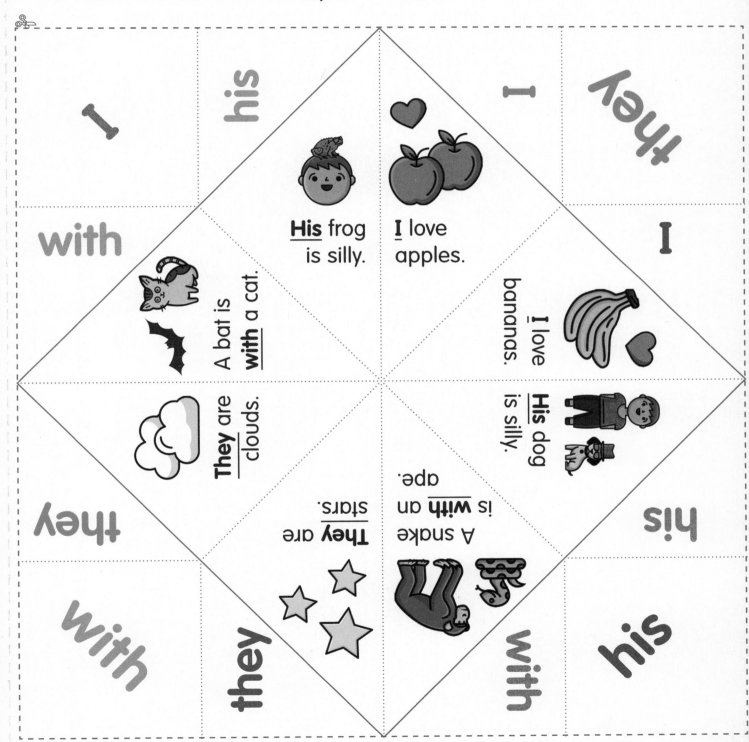

His frog is silly.

I love apples.

A bat is **with** a cat.

They are clouds.

I love bananas.

His dog is silly.

A snake is **with** an ape.

They are stars.

I

his

they

with

I

they

his

with

his

Words to Know

Grown-up: Say the words aloud in a normal voice. Then invite your child to say the words in a silly voice.

this

be

at

have

Say them in a *football player* voice!

Word Practice

Trace.

We have fun **at** the pool.

Write.

Circle each **at**. (Hint: There are 6.)

c	m	w	e	h	r	a	t	f	y
g	l	u	d	o	q	n	k	m	a
a	z	n	f	r	s	p	i	x	t
t	r	x	a	t	h	w	j	c	b
v	k	h	e	u	z	a	v	g	l
s	o	p	i	b	j	t	d	a	t

Scholastic Inc.

Word Practice

Trace.

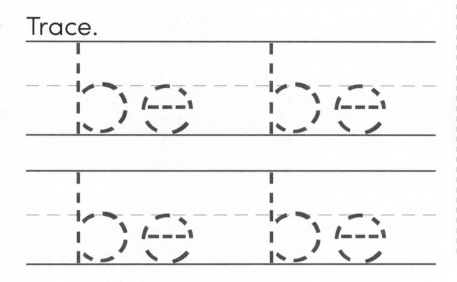

I want to **be** a chef.

Write.

Help the girl shoot a basket. Color the balls with **be**.

Scholastic Inc.

Word Practice

Trace.

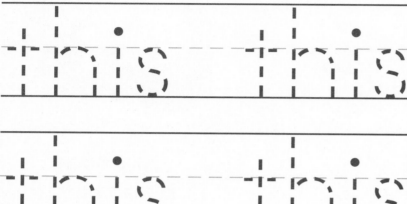

This is Rob and Dan. They are twins.

Write.

Find each **this**. Color that space **brown**. Then color the rest of the picture.

Word Practice

Trace.

have

have

Can I **have** a pet snake?

Write.

Find each **have**. Color that space **green**. Then color the rest of the picture.

What's Missing?

Fill in the boxes to make words from the list.

1. t ☐ i s

2. a ☐

3. ☐ e

4. h a ☐ e

Word List
at
be
this
have

Complete the sentences. Use the word list.

1. I want to _____ an acrobat.

2. Look at _____ picture of me.

3. Look _____ them build.

4. I _____ brown hair.

Sight Word Maze

Help Mr. Rat find his friend Mr. Cat. Find each **have**.
Color that space **green**.

Start				
have	at	be	this	at
have	have	have	have	have
be	at	this	at	have
have	have	have	have	have
have	be	at	this	be
have	have	this	be	at
at	have	have	have	this

End

Word Sort

Cut out the flowers on page 79.
Sort them onto the stems.

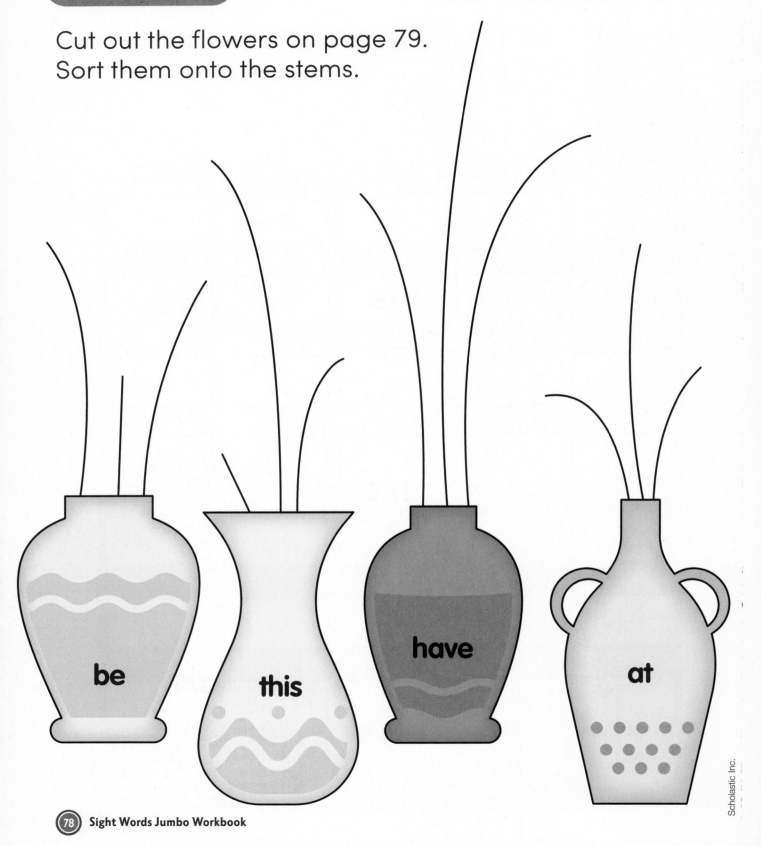

Scholastic Inc.

Sight Word Catcher

Cut and fold the Fun Flap.

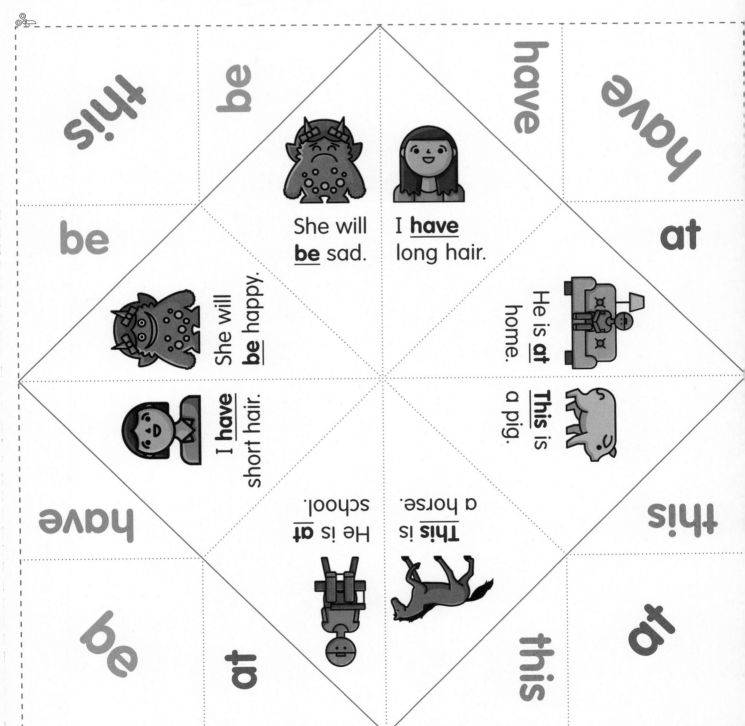

She will **be** sad.

I **have** long hair.

She will **be** happy.

He is **at** home.

I **have** short hair.

This is a pig.

He is **at** school.

This is a horse.

Words to Know

Grown-up: Say the words aloud in a normal voice. Then invite your child to say the words in a silly voice.

one

or

from

had

Say them in a pirate voice!

Word Practice

Trace.

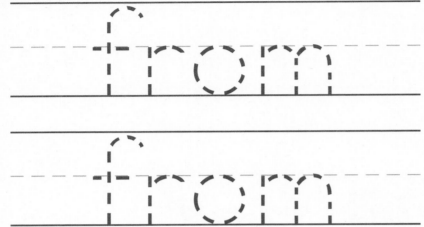

It is
from China.

Write.

Find each **from**. Color that penguin **tan**.
Then color the rest of the picture.

Scholastic Inc.

Word Practice

Trace.

Do you like snakes **or** snails?

Write.

Find each **or**. Color that space **purple**.
Then color the rest of the picture.

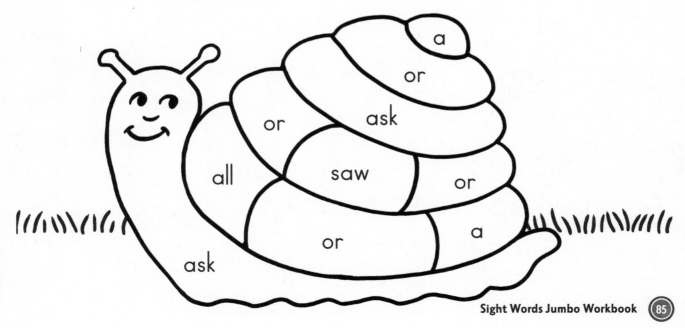

Scholastic Inc.

Word Practice

Trace.

I only have **one** shoe.

Write.

Circle each **one**. (Hint: There are 6.)

f a k b o r s n o p
g t d v o n e l n m
o n e c f a x i e z
w n q o k o n e c o
y l z n r t w m g n
o n e j d i q r s e

Word Practice

Trace.

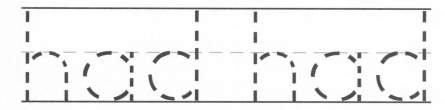

We **had** pizza for lunch.

Write.

Find each **had**. Color that ball yellow.
Then color the rest of the picture.

add

 had

he

had

 dad

 had

 had

ham

What's Missing?

Fill in the boxes to make words from the list.

1. o ☐ e

2. ☐ r

3. f ☐ o m

4. h a ☐

Word List
from
or
one
had

Complete the sentences. Use the word list.

1. She will get gifts _____ her friends.

2. Do you want to draw _____ read?

3. I see _____ dog.

4. They _____ fun at the party.

Scholastic Inc.

Tic-Tac Sight Word

Play the games below. The word with three Xs or Os wins!

Place an **X** over **from**.
(Circle) **or**.

from	or	or
from	from	from
or	from	or

This word won: _____

Place an **X** over **one**.
(Circle) **had**.

had	had	one
had	one	had
one	had	one

This word won: _____

Place an **X** over **from**.
(Circle) **had**.

had	from	from
from	had	had
had	from	had

This word won: _____

Place an **X** over **one**.
(Circle) **or**.

one	or	or
or	or	one
or	one	one

This word won: _____

Word Sort

Cut out the bows on page 91.
Sort them onto the kite strings.

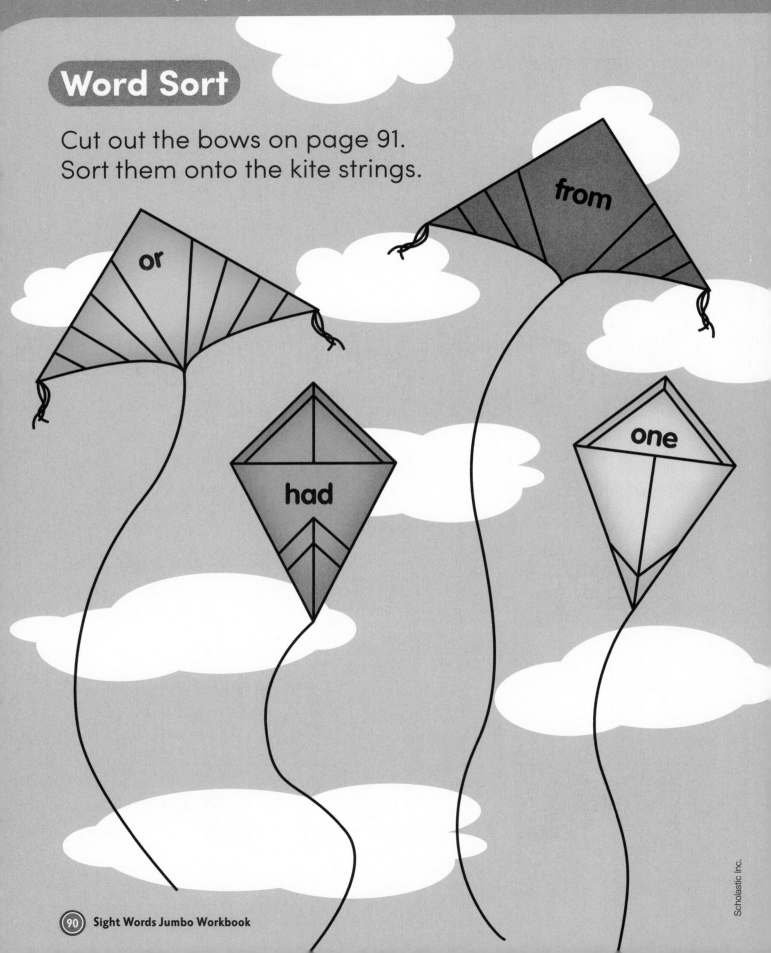

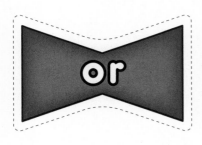

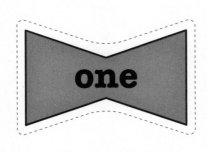

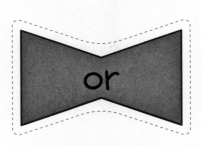

Sight Word Catcher

Cut and fold the Fun Flap.

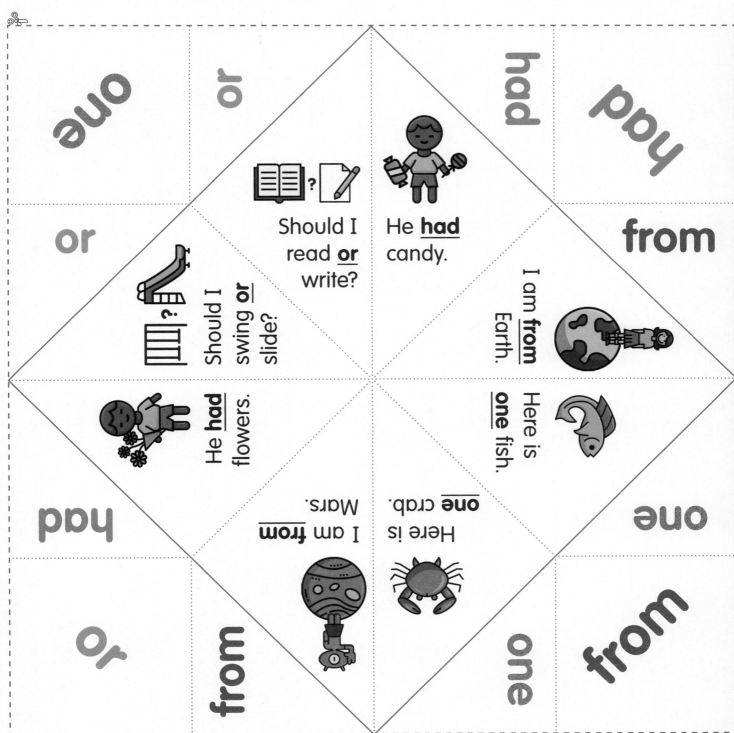

Words to Know

Grown-up: Say the words aloud in a normal voice. Then invite your child to say the words in a silly voice.

by

words

not

but

Say them in a dinosaur voice!

Word Practice

Trace.

by by

by by

This book is **by** my favorite author.

Write.

Find each **by**. Color that shape yellow.
Then color the rest of the picture.

but
but

by

buy

by

by

but

by

bye

but

Word Practice

Trace.

words

words

I like the **words**
elegant and *elephant*.

Write.

Find each **words**.
Color that space **purple**.
Then color the rest
of the picture.

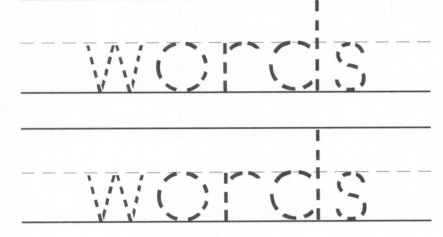

won

words

wore

words

worn

ward

words

worn

words

Word Practice

Trace.

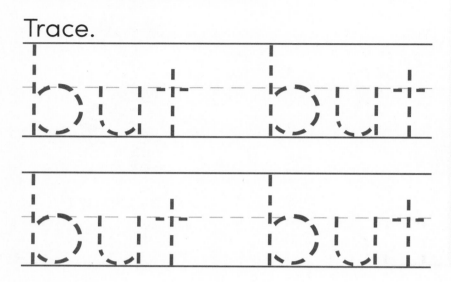

My dog is small **but** loud.

Write.

Find each **but**. Color that space **blue**. Then color the rest of the picture.

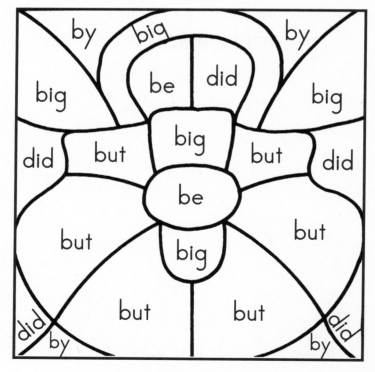

Word Practice

Trace.

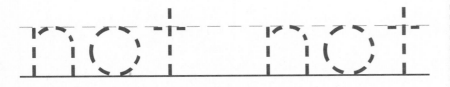

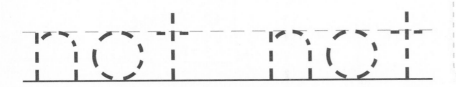

The rain will **not** stop.

Write.

Circle each **not**. (Hint: There are 6.)

v a d k i n w x n m
g n o t c o u r o h
l w x s f t e b t z
j b n u n o t p c s
y e o m i l v f g d
p h t r q a b n o t

What's Missing?

Fill in the boxes to make words from the list.

1. w o ☐ d s

2. ☐ o t

3. b ☐ t

4. ☐ y

○ Word List
    by
○   words
    but
○   not

Complete the sentences. Use the word list.

1. Jen does _____ like bugs.

2. Yumi writes the _____ on the board.

3. She is _____ the tree.

4. I have paper _____ no pencil.

Scholastic Inc.

Sight Word Color

Color the picture. Use the Color Key.

Color Key	
words	Green
by	Pink
but	Purple
not	Yellow

Word Sort

Cut out the bubbles on page 103.
Sort them above the bubble wands.

words   but   by   not

Scholastic Inc.

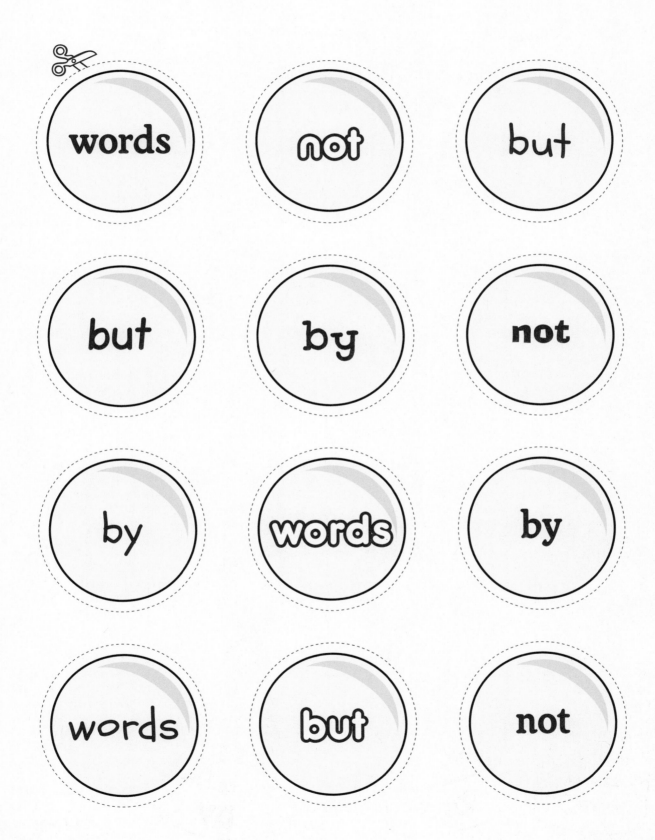

Sight Word Catcher

Cut and fold the Fun Flap.

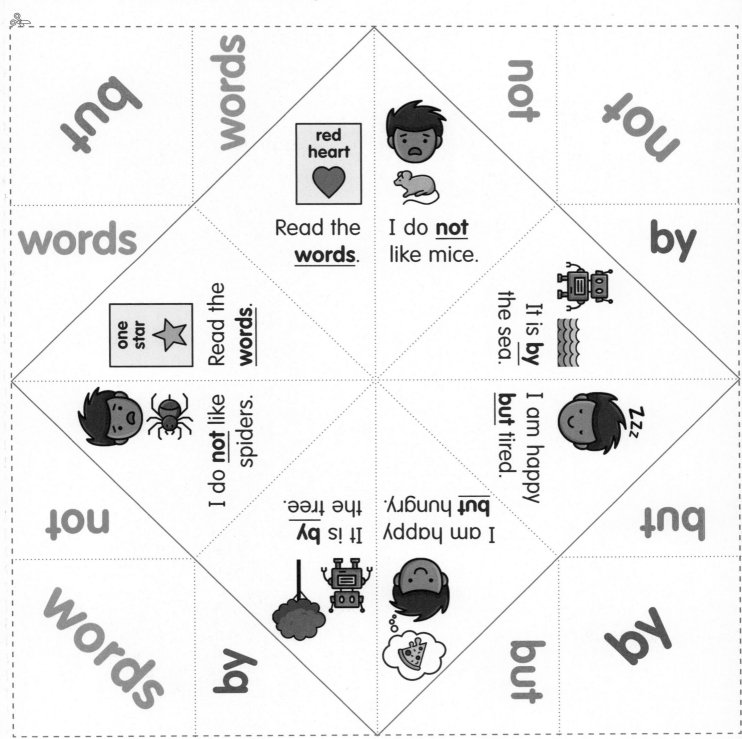

Words to Know

Grown-up: Say the words aloud in a normal voice. Then invite your child to say the words in a silly voice.

what

were

we

all

Say them in an owl voice!

Word Practice

Trace.

Do you know **what** is in here?

Write.

Circle each **what**. (Hint: There are 6.)

y	l	e	v	s	b	w	h	a	t
d	w	h	a	t	i	f	c	r	w
w	f	q	u	z	l	n	w	g	h
h	n	k	r	o	x	e	h	o	a
a	g	w	h	a	t	u	a	m	t
t	c	p	j	i	d	q	t	s	v

Word Practice

Trace.

all all

all all

The lion has **all** the lollipops.

Write.

Find each **all**. Color that space **red**.
Then color the rest of the picture.

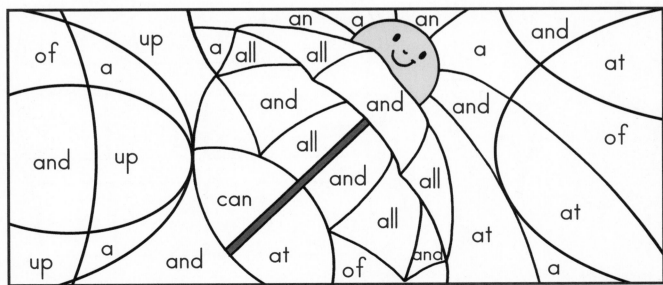

Word Practice

Trace.

The frogs **were** on a log.

Write.

Find each **were**. Color that space **blue**. Then color the rest of the picture.

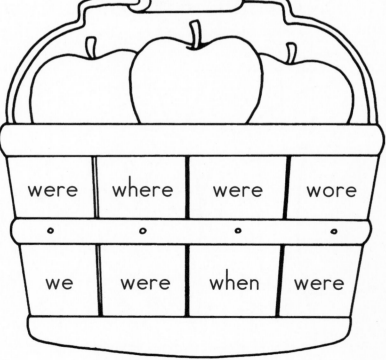

| were | where | were | wore |
| we | were | when | were |

Word Practice

Trace.

I hope **we** see a whale.

Write.

Circle each **we**. (Hint: There are 6.)

v	f	c	z	b	w	e	x	u	g
m	a	z	i	h	p	q	r	j	w
s	w	e	g	t	l	n	w	k	e
j	o	x	v	u	a	f	e	i	d
b	h	w	c	y	w	e	l	m	o
f	r	e	d	k	q	t	s	p	n

What's Missing?

Fill in the boxes to make words from the list.

1. w ☐ a t

2. ☐ l l

3. w ☐

4. w e ☐ e

o Word List
  what
o were
  all
o we

~~~~~~~~~~~~~~~~~~~~~~~~~~~~~~~~~~

Complete the sentences. Use the word list.

1. Do you know _____ you want to do?

2. Did your cat sleep _____ day?

3. Where should _____ go now?

4. They _____ ready to leave.

Scholastic Inc.

Sight Word Maze

Help the mole find its way above ground.
Find the tunnel with the word **we**.

Word Sort

Cut out the bugs on page 115.
Sort them onto the leaves.

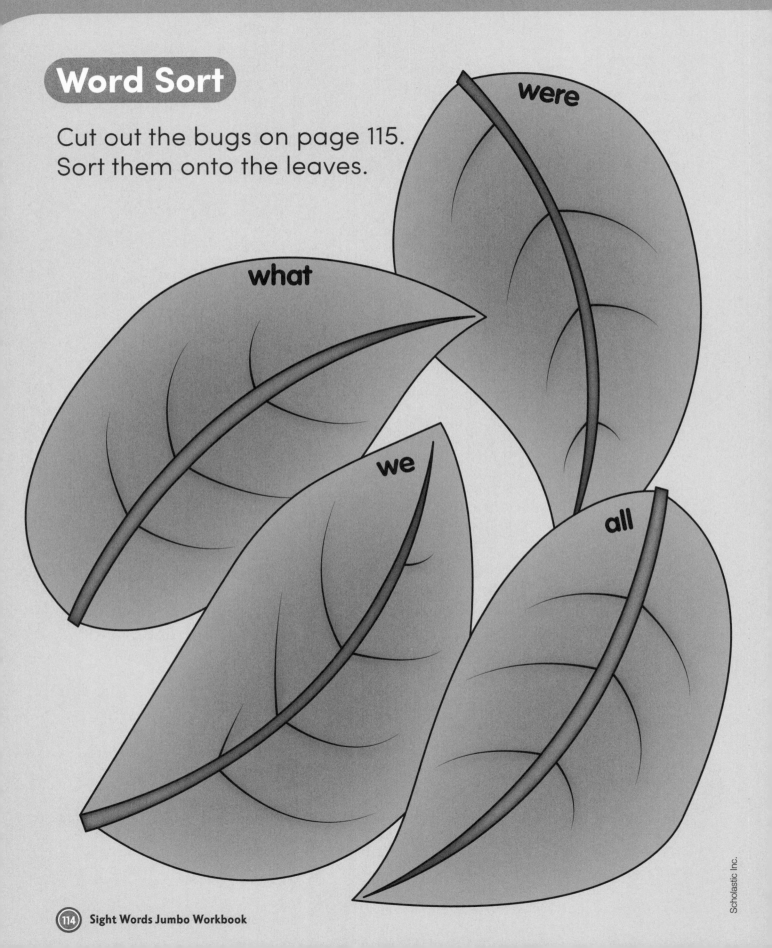

Sight Words Jumbo Workbook

Sight Word Catcher

Cut and fold the Fun Flap.

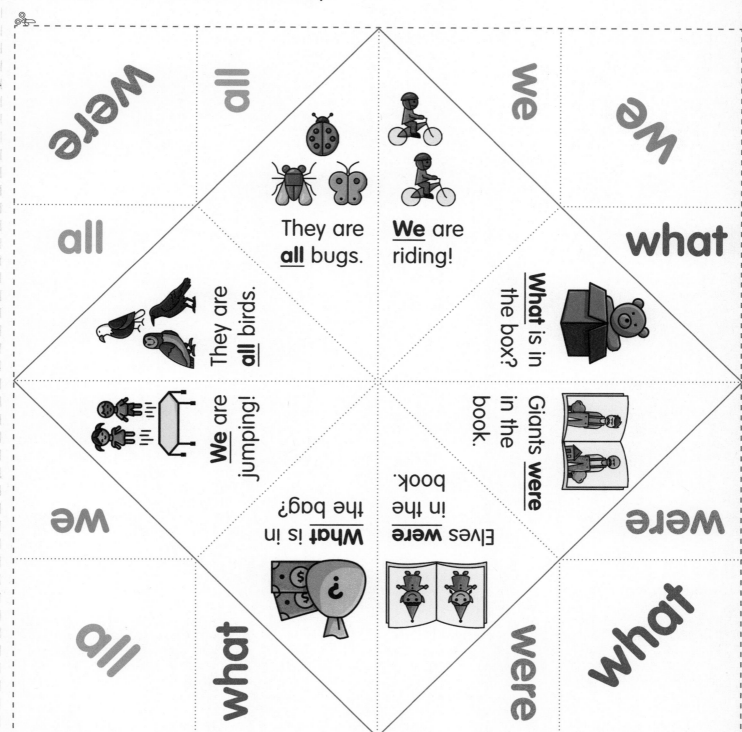

They are **all** bugs.

We are riding!

They are **all** birds.

We are jumping!

What is in the box?

Giants **were** in the book.

Elves **were** in the book.

What is in the bag?

Words to Know

Grown-up: Say the words aloud in a normal voice. Then invite your child to say the words in a silly voice.

can

your

when

said

Say them in a *ghost* voice!

Word Practice

Trace.

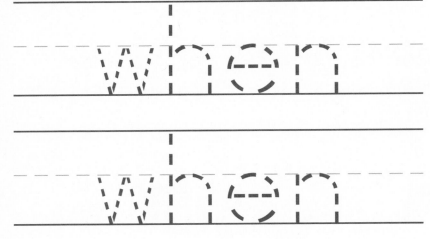

I eat **when**
I am hungry.

Write.

Find each **when**. Color that pie **brown**.
Then color the rest of the picture.

Scholastic Inc.

Word Practice

Trace.

your

your

It is **your** book.

Write.

Find each **your**. Color that puff **red**.
Then color the rest of the picture.

your

your

our

four

you

your

your

joy

Word Practice

Trace.

I **can** jump rope!

Write.

Circle each **can**. (Hint: There are 6.)

f	p	k	v	e	c	o	m	s	l
c	b	t	d	g	a	u	c	a	n
a	l	o	h	j	n	x	i	t	r
n	i	c	a	n	p	k	f	b	c
j	u	m	e	r	c	a	n	t	a
v	g	s	y	d	z	q	w	h	n

Word Practice

Trace.

Mom **said** she likes the flower.

Write.

Find each **said**. Color those butterflies **purple**. Then color the rest of the picture.

so

said

saw

said

was

saw

said

saw

What's Missing?

Fill in the boxes to make words from the list.

Word List
when
your
can
said

1. w h ☐ n

2. c ☐ n

3. s ☐ i d

4. ☐ o u r

Complete the sentences. Use the word list.

1. "Hello," _____ the teacher.

2. I smile _____ I am happy.

3. Take off _____ hat.

4. Dorian _____ go with his father.

Scholastic Inc.

Tic-Tac Sight Word

Play the games below. The word with three **X**s or **O**s wins!

Place an **X** over **when**.
(Circle) **your**.

when	your	when
your	when	your
your	your	when

This word won: _____

Place an **X** over **can**.
(Circle) **said**.

said	said	can
can	can	said
can	said	can

This word won: _____

Place an **X** over **when**.
(Circle) **said**.

when	said	when
said	said	said
said	when	when

This word won: _____

Place an **X** over **can**.
(Circle) **your**.

your	can	can
your	your	can
can	can	your

This word won: _____

Word Sort

Cut out the fish on page 127. Sort them into the pond.

when   your   can   said

Scholastic Inc.

Sight Word Catcher

Cut and fold the Fun Flap.

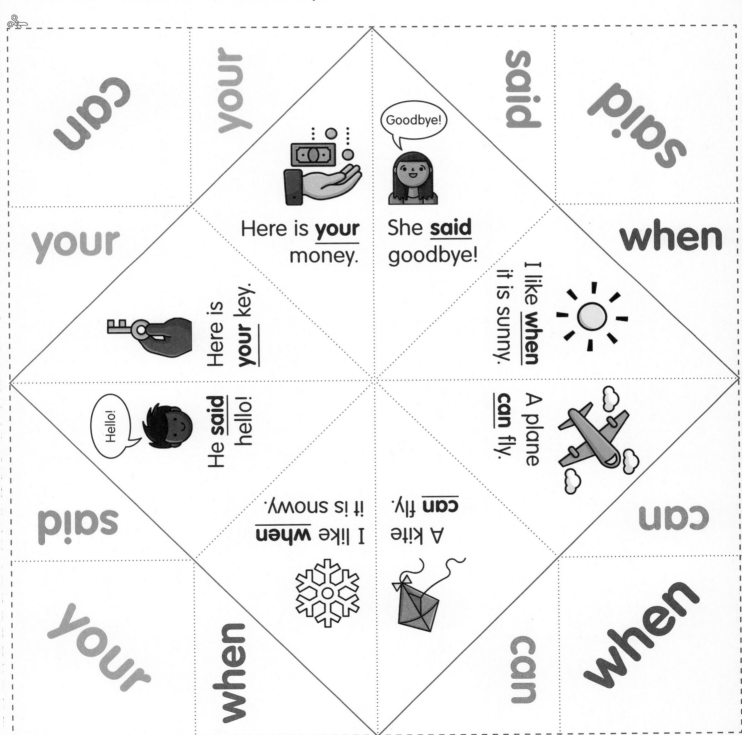

Words to Know

Grown-up: Say the words aloud in a normal voice. Then invite your child to say the words in a silly voice.

use

there

each

an

Say them in a monkey voice!

Word Practice

Trace.

t̲h̲e̲r̲e̲

t̲h̲e̲r̲e̲

My kite
is **there**.

Write.

Find each **there**. Color that space **brown**.
Then color the rest of the picture.

there

then

there

which   the

them

there

then   the

which

which   there

Word Practice

Trace.

Can I **use** them?

Write.

Find each **use**. Color that snowflake **blue**.
Then color the rest of the picture.

us   use   use   us

you   use   you   use

Word Practice

Trace.

An elephant
is big!

Write.

Find each **an**. Color that leaf **orange**.
Then color the rest of the picture.

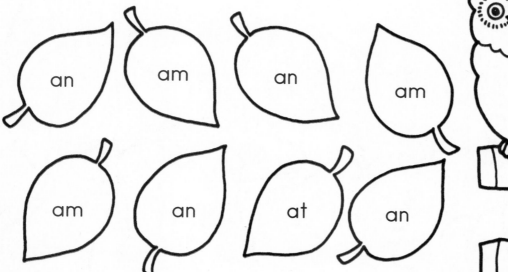

an   am   an   am

am   an   at   an

Word Practice

Trace.

each

each

I want one
of **each**!

Write.

Find each **each**.
Color that shape brown.
Then color the rest
of the picture.

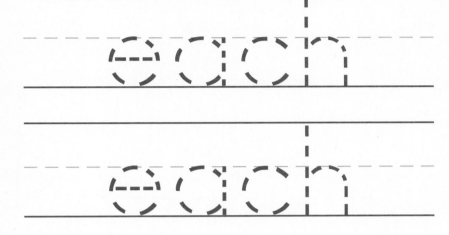

each

at

each

eat

each

at

each

each

each

What's Missing?

Fill in the boxes to make words from the list.

1. u ☐ e

2. e a ☐ h

3. t ☐ e r e

4. ☐ n

Word List
there
use
an
each

Complete the sentences. Use the word list.

1. Look over _____!

2. The boy has _____ apple.

3. I have five fingers on _____ hand.

4. I _____ crayons to color.

Scholastic Inc.

Sight Word Maze

Help the bus get to the school. Connect a path by coloring each box with a list word.

Word List

there	an
use	each

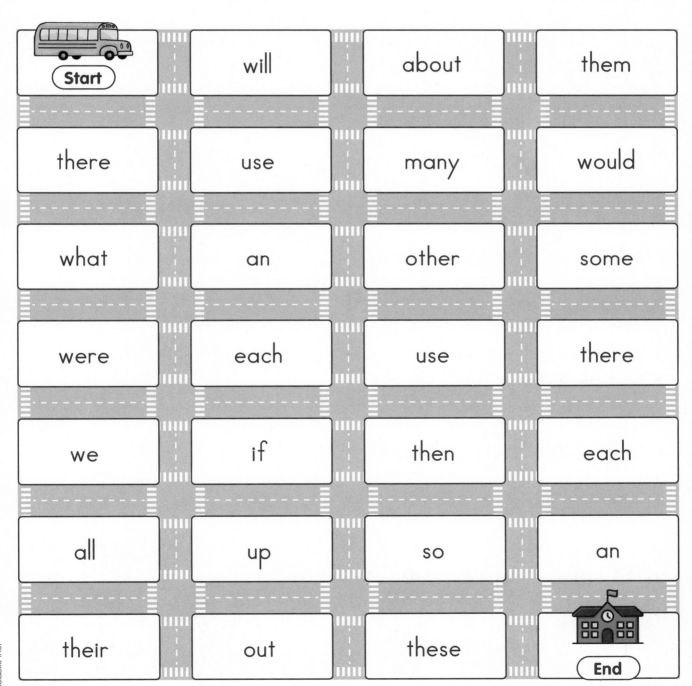

Start	will	about	them
there	use	many	would
what	an	other	some
were	each	use	there
we	if	then	each
all	up	so	an
their	out	these	End

Word Sort

Cut out the seashells on page 139.
Sort them onto the sand.

Scholastic Inc.

 each

 there

 each

 an

 there

 an

 use

 use

 there

 use

 an

 each

Scholastic Inc.

Sight Word Catcher

Cut and fold the Fun Flap.

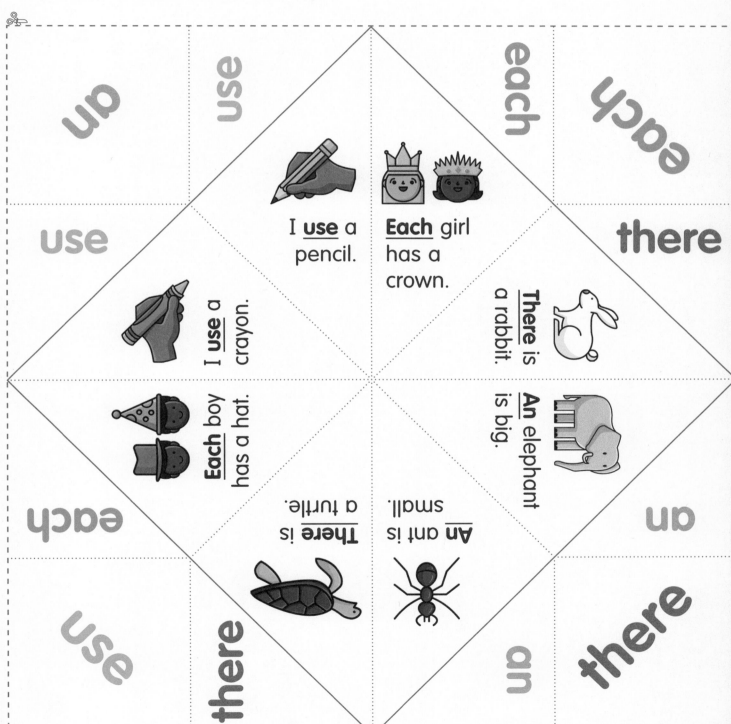

Words to Know

Grown-up: Say the words aloud in a normal voice. Then invite your child to say the words in a silly voice.

which

she

how

do

Say them in a mermaid voice!

Word Practice

Trace.

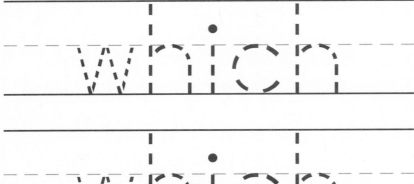

Which dog is barking?

Write.

Find each **which**. Color that treat **red**.
Then color the rest of the picture.

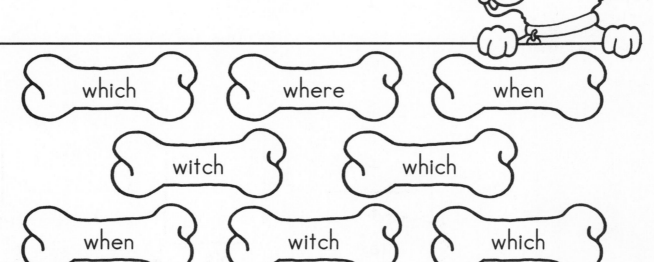

which	where	when
	witch	which
when	witch	which

Word Practice

Trace.

she   she

she   she

I hope **she** likes the gift.

Write.

Find each **she**. Color that space **green**. Then color the rest of the picture.

she

her   shoe

he

the   she   the

he   see

she   his   she

Word Practice

Trace.

d o   d o

d o   d o

Pick one of these to **do**.

Write.

Circle each **do**. (Hint: There are 6.)

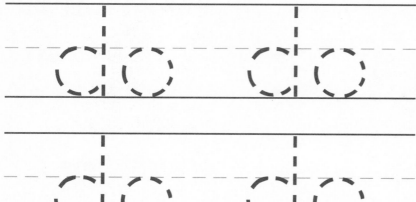

t	y	j	t	r	a	d	o	h	i
m	f	q	c	v	g	u	l	s	d
z	u	w	d	o	n	p	e	t	o
v	d	e	a	k	x	m	d	b	c
l	o	h	b	i	t	r	o	g	k
s	n	p	y	f	d	o	w	q	x

Scholastic Inc.

Word Practice

Trace.

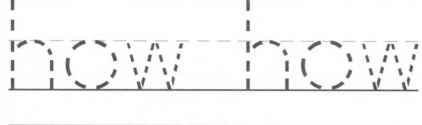

Hello, **how** are you?

Write.

Find each **how**. Color that space **orange**. Then color the rest of the picture.

how

how

wow

how

row

owl

how

how

how

how

Scholastic Inc.

What's Missing?

Fill in the boxes to make words from the list.

1. d ☐

2. s h ☐

3. w ☐ i c h

4. ☐ o w

○ Word List
which
she
do
how

Complete the sentences. Use the word list.

1. How will you choose _____ one to take?

2. Did _____ play with her puppy?

3. Let's _____ a dance.

4. See _____ they play.

Sight Word Maze

Help the school bus get to the school.
Find the street with the word **which**.

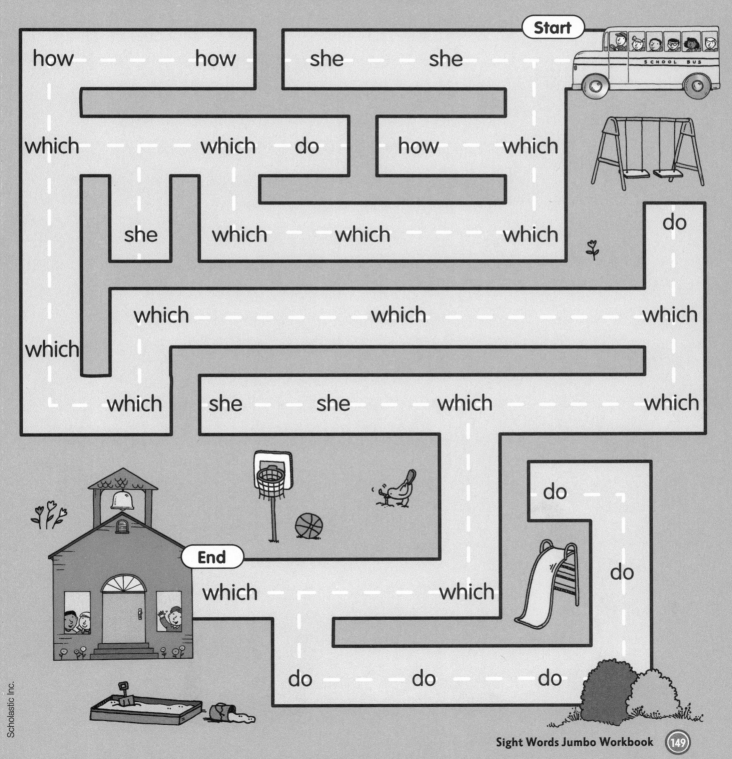

Scholastic Inc.

Word Sort

Cut out the balls on page 151.
Stack them on top of the seals' noses.

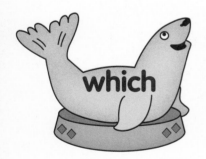

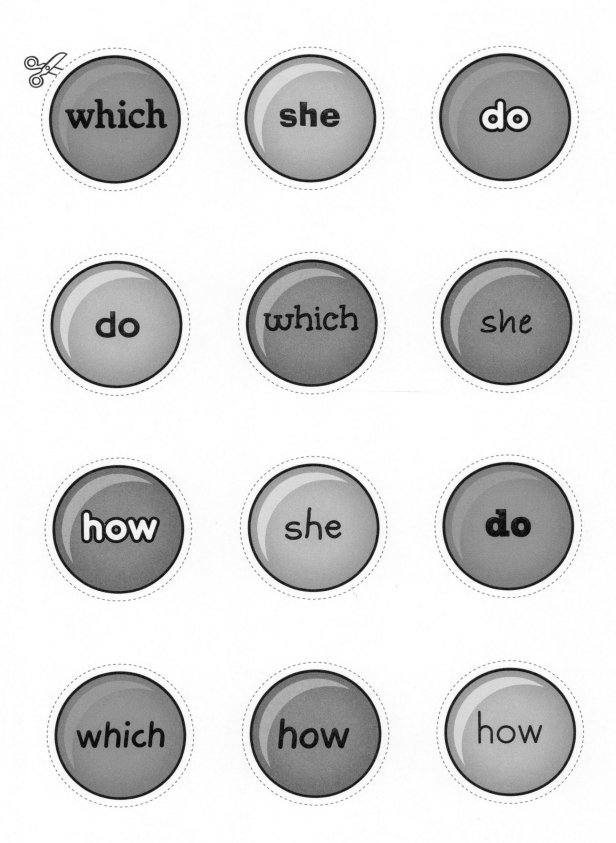

Sight Word Catcher

Cut and fold the Fun Flap.

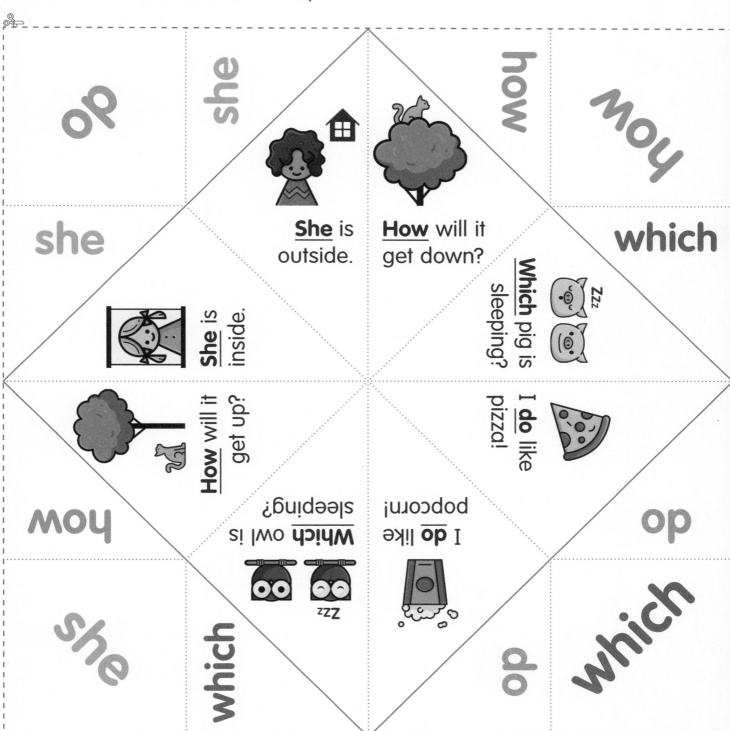

Words to Know

Grown-up: Say the words aloud in a normal voice. Then invite your child to say the words in a silly voice.

will

if

their

up

Say them in a Frankenstein voice!

SWEETS

Word Practice

Trace.

their

their

I like **their** wigs!

Write.

Find each **their**. Color that space **purple**.
Then color the rest of the picture.

Scholastic Inc.

Word Practice

Trace.

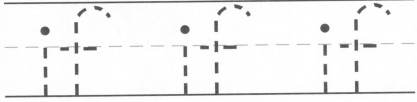

Let's see **if** it will float.

Write.

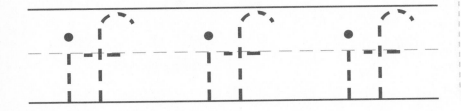

Help the frog find the log. Color the lily pads with **if**.

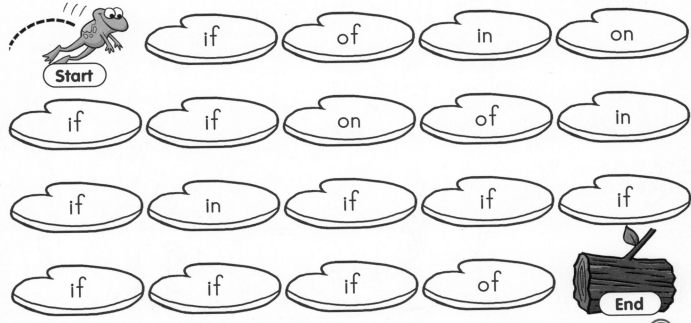

Word Practice

Trace.

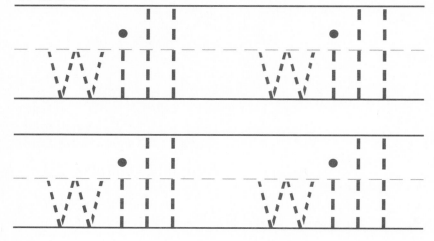

Will you read
me this story?

Write.

Find each **will**. Color that space **black**. Then color the rest of the picture.

Scholastic Inc.

Word Practice

Trace.

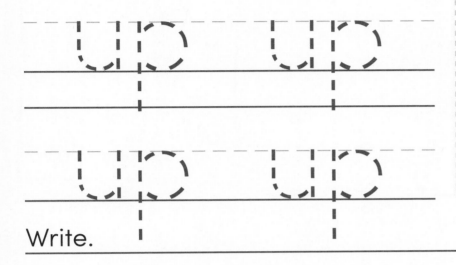

Write.

The plane can fly **up** high.

Circle each **up**. (Hint: There are 6.)

t	v	k	u	o	r	n	u	p	f
g	a	q	p	c	h	s	l	m	q
d	u	n	b	f	u	r	i	j	r
z	p	s	a	v	p	y	u	p	b
y	l	h	e	t	z	w	o	g	k
w	u	p	j	d	i	q	c	x	e

What's Missing?

Fill in the boxes to make words from the list.

1. w i ☐ l

2. ☐ f

3. t ☐ e i r

4. u ☐

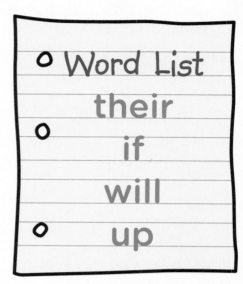

o Word List
their
o if
will
o up

Complete the sentences. Use the word list.

1. The cat jumps _____ .

2. The kids do _____ work.

3. Where _____ we go for dinner?

4. I wonder _____ he will be home.

Scholastic Inc.

Tic-Tac Sight Word

Play the games below. The word with three Xs or Os wins!

Place an **X** over **their**.
(Circle) **if**.

if	their	their
if	if	if
their	if	their

This word won: _____

Place an **X** over **will**.
(Circle) **up**.

up	will	up
will	up	will
will	will	up

This word won: _____

Place an **X** over **their**.
(Circle) **up**.

up	up	their
up	their	up
their	up	their

This word won: _____

Place an **X** over **will**.
(Circle) **if**.

if	will	will
will	if	will
if	if	will

This word won: _____

Word Sort

Cut out the biscuits. Sort them into the dog bowls.

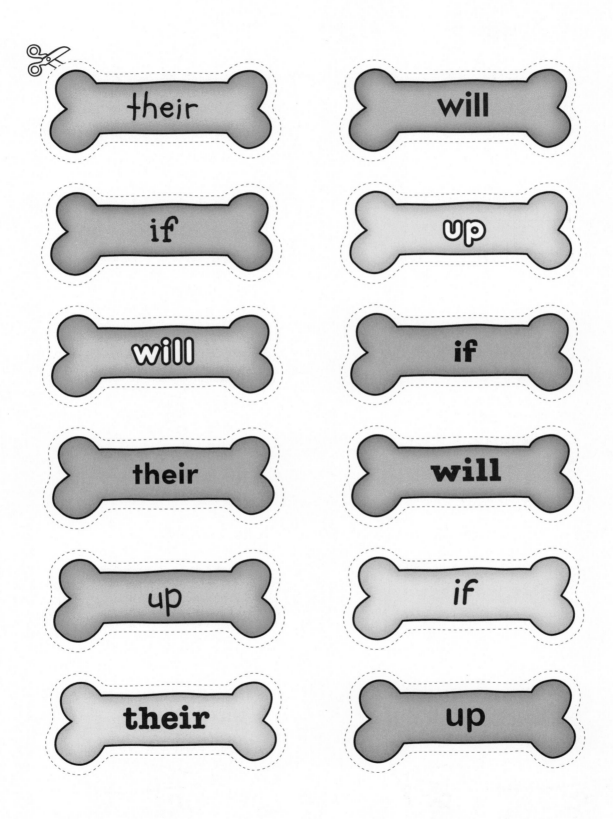

Sight Word Catcher

Cut and fold the Fun Flap.

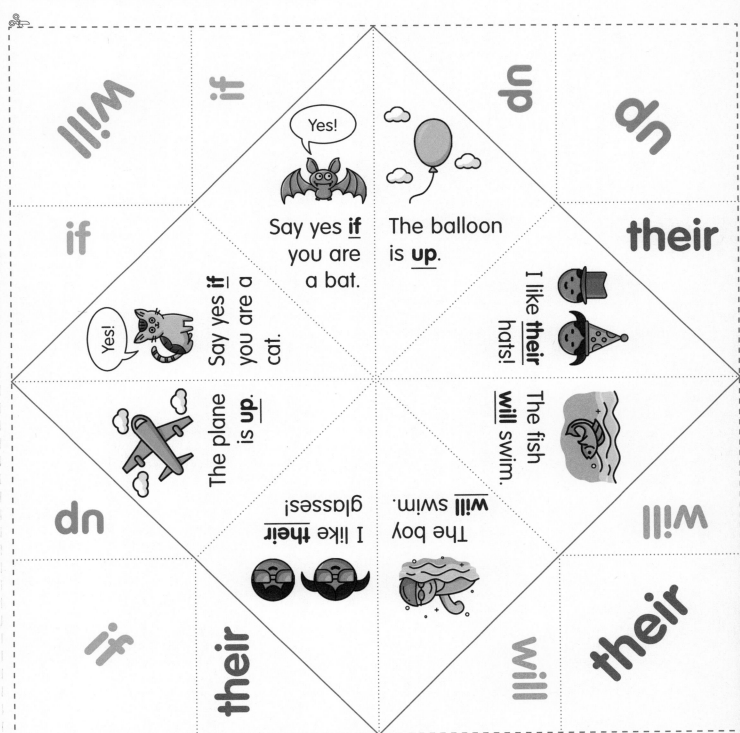

Words to Know

Grown-up: Say the words aloud in a normal voice. Then invite your child to say the words in a silly voice.

out

about

other

many

Say them in a *boat captain* voice!

Word Practice

Trace.

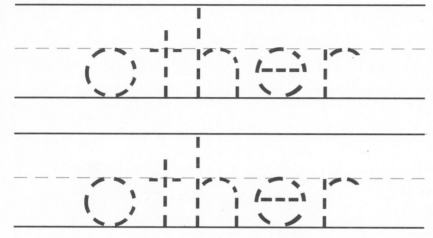

I want the **other** book.

Write.

Find each **other**. Color that star yellow.
Then color the rest of the picture.

air

am

other

arm

other

other

art

other

Word Practice

Trace.

about

about

This show is **about** dinosaurs.

Write.

Find each **about**. Color that rocket **blue**.
Then color the rest of the picture.

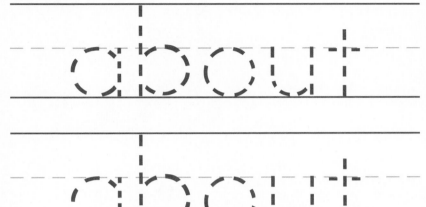

Word Practice

Trace.

The owl comes **out** at night.

Write.

Circle each **out**. (Hint: There are 6.)

e	a	k	w	r	o	u	t	i	o
g	f	c	x	j	m	l	d	q	u
n	o	u	t	s	w	o	h	p	t
b	r	d	p	o	a	u	f	e	s
q	l	i	z	u	b	t	o	u	t
v	h	m	j	t	n	c	g	y	k

Word Practice

Trace.

I like **many** kinds of sweets!

Write.

Find each **many**. Color that muffin yellow.
Then color the rest of the picture.

What's Missing?

Fill in the boxes to make words from the list.

1. m ☐ n y

2. a b ☐ u t

3. ☐ t h e r

4. o u ☐

Word List

other

about

out

many

Complete the sentences. Use the word list.

1. Read _____ history.

2. How _____ soccer balls did you kick?

3. The cat gets _____ of the box.

4. Help me find the _____ sock.

Sight Word Maze

Help the miner find the jewels.
Find the path with the word **many**.

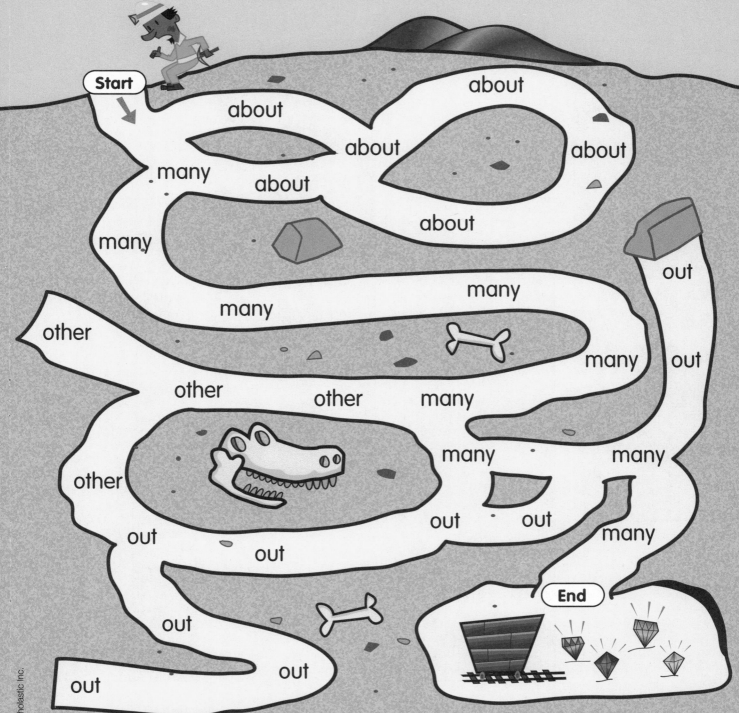

Word Sort

Cut out the bows on page 175.
Sort them onto the presents.

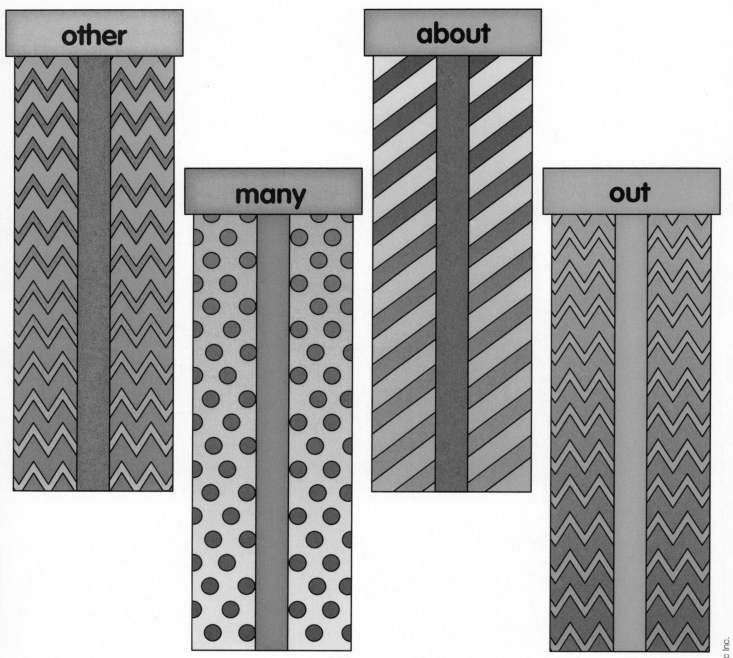

Scholastic Inc.

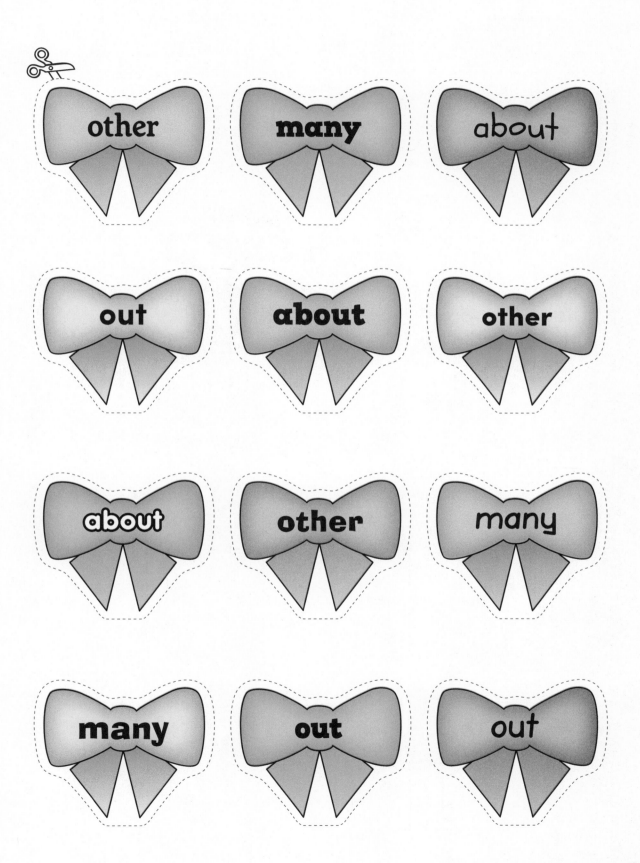

other

many

about

out

about

other

about

other

many

many

out

out

Sight Word Catcher

Cut and fold the Fun Flap.

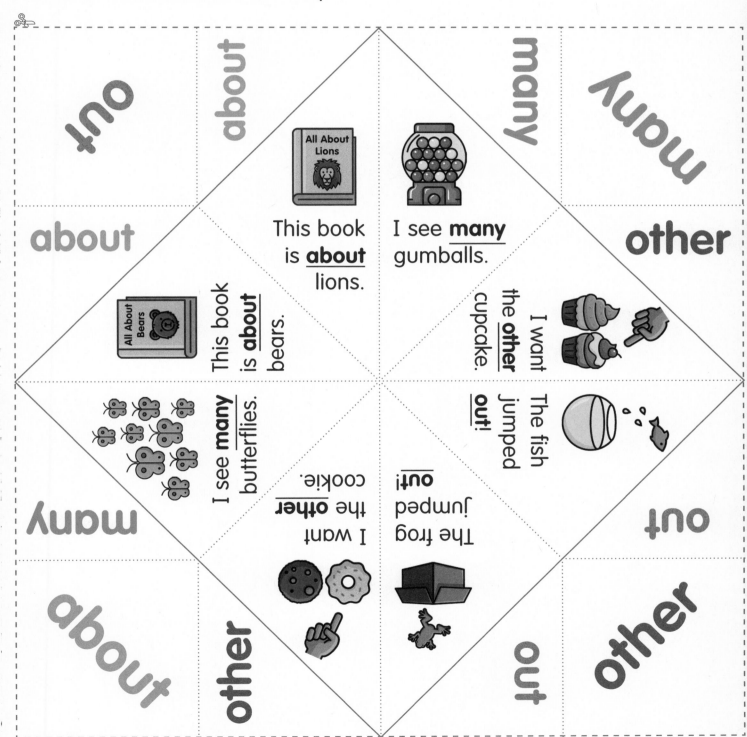

Words to Know

Grown-up: Say the words aloud in a normal voice. Then invite your child to say the words in a silly voice.

then

so

these

them

Say them in a *goblin* voice!

Word Practice

Trace.

then

then

She shopped and **then** went home.

Write.

Circle each **then**. (Hint: There are 6.)

b	a	t	l	p	f	y	d	u	c
g	s	h	x	t	h	e	n	m	o
t	d	e	k	q	u	z	i	t	v
h	c	n	m	v	r	a	b	h	p
e	t	h	e	n	s	w	f	e	l
n	o	r	t	h	e	n	g	n	j

Scholastic Inc.

Word Practice

Trace.

t h e m

t h e m

I pet
them both.

Write.

Find each **them**. Color that space **green**.
Then color the rest of the picture.

the   then   he   them   the
them   them   they
them   them   the
to   them   that
them   then   the
the   to   to   to

Word Practice

Trace.

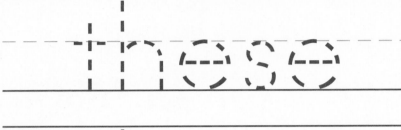

These jeans
are blue.

Write.

Find each **these**. Color that space **brown**. Then color the rest of the picture.

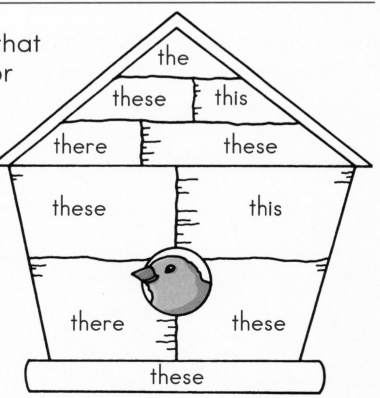

the

these | this

there | these

these | this

there | these

these

Scholastic Inc.

Word Practice

Trace.

The snail is **so** slow.

Write.

Circle each **so**. (Hint: There are 6.)

b	r	x	a	s	p	m	l	z	g
t	s	o	f	o	y	n	e	h	k
g	d	u	w	b	c	i	s	o	m
v	p	x	j	d	k	q	r	v	s
s	o	c	n	l	s	f	u	t	o
y	k	h	e	z	o	w	a	b	q

What's Missing?

Fill in the boxes to make words from the list.

1. t h ☐ n

2. t ☐ e m

3. t h e ☐ e

4. ☐ o

Word List
then
them
these
so

~~~~~~~~~~~~~~~~~~~~

Complete the sentences. Use the word list.

1. Julia made _____ cupcakes.

2. I read and _____ sleep.

3. His cat is _____ fluffy.

4. Look at _____ play.

Sight Word Color

Color the picture. Use the Color Key.

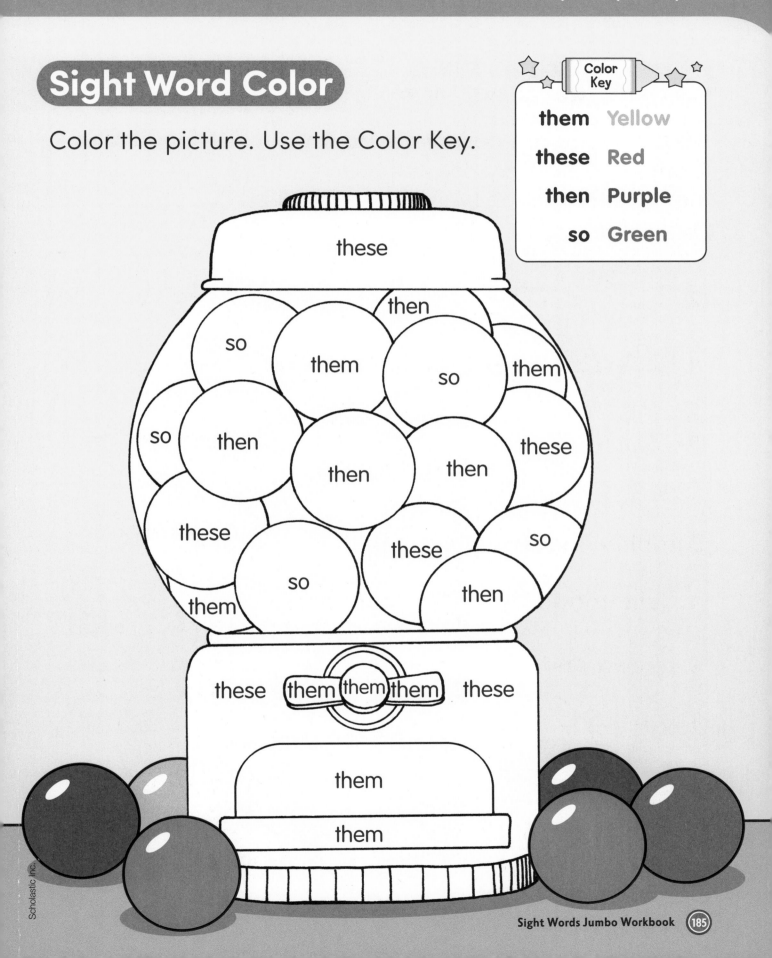

Color Key

them	Yellow
these	Red
then	Purple
so	Green

Sight Word Maze

Word List

Help the squirrel collect the acorns. Connect a path by coloring each box with a list word.

then	these
them	so

Start

will	out	if
then	their	about	all
so	them	if	out
what	then	these	each
can	many	then	so
said	other	up	End

Scholastic Inc.

Sight Word Catcher

Cut and fold the Fun Flap.

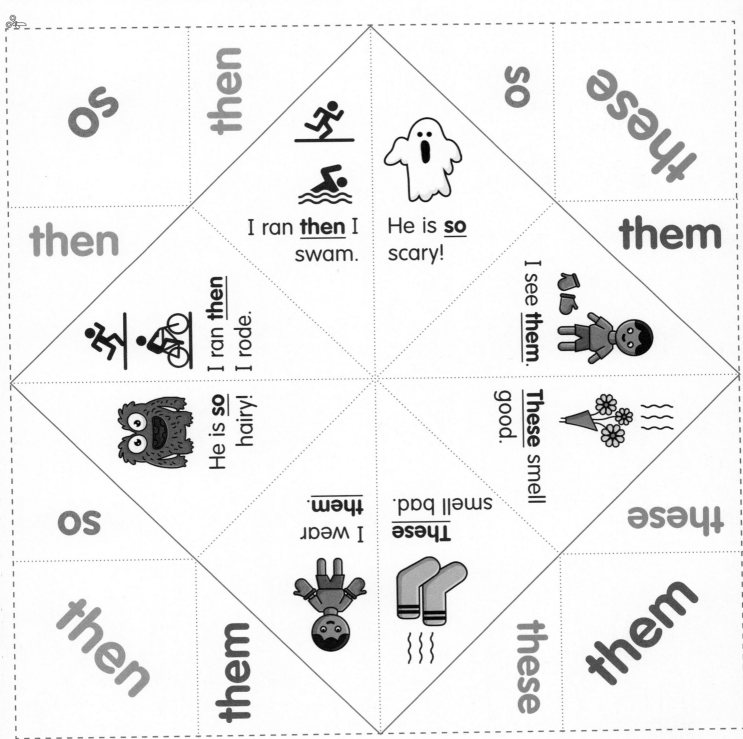

Words to Know

Grown-up: Say the words aloud in a normal voice. Then invite your child to say the words in a silly voice.

would

her

some

make

Say them in a *sloth* voice!

Word Practice

Trace.

Do you want **some** popcorn?

Write.

Circle each **some**. (Hint: There are 6.)

c	u	q	s	r	k	n	l	p	z
s	w	g	o	w	d	s	o	m	e
o	t	z	m	v	s	r	i	t	j
m	i	b	e	x	o	a	f	g	n
e	p	h	j	l	m	s	o	m	e
s	o	m	e	d	e	k	u	y	v

Word Practice

Trace.

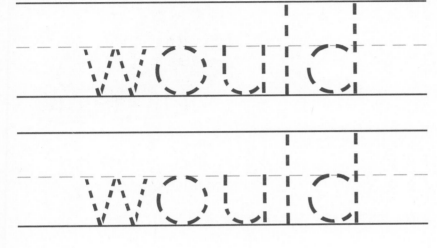

Would you like pizza?

Write.

Find each **would**. Color that sail **purple**.
Then color the rest of the picture.

Word Practice

Trace.

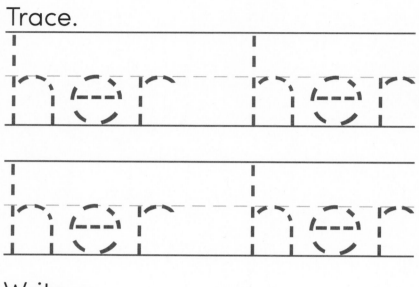

The girl played on **her** slide.

Write.

Circle each **her**. (Hint: There are 6.)

q h e r o z p y a h
g t u v c i n l m e
n h s k h e r j t r
f e x a m q v h s b
y r w h e r u e k g
t l o j d b p r c f

Word Practice

Trace.

make

make

We can **make** a cake!

Write.

_____

Find each **where**. Color that space **yellow**. Then color the rest of the picture.

take

rake

take

make

lake

make

fake

make

lake

fake

rake

make

What's Missing?

Fill in the boxes to make words from the list.

Word List
some
her
would
make

1. w o ☐ l d

2. m ☐ k e

3. ☐ e r

4. s o m ☐

Complete the sentences. Use the word list.

1. We _____ dinner together.

2. I like _____ jacket.

3. Do you want _____ milk and cookies?

4. I _____ like to dance.

MILK

Scholastic Inc.

Tic-Tac Sight Word

Play the games below. The word with three Xs or Os wins!

Place an **X** over **some**.
(Circle) **her**.

her	some	some
her	some	her
her	her	some

This word won: _____

Place an **X** over **would**.
(Circle) **make**.

would	make	make
make	make	would
would	make	would

This word won: _____

Place an **X** over **some**.
(Circle) **make**.

make	some	some
make	some	make
some	make	make

This word won: _____

Place an **X** over **would**.
(Circle) **her**.

would	would	her
her	would	her
would	her	would

This word won: _____

Word Sort

Cut out the pigs on page 197.
Sort them into the mud puddles.

her

make

would

some

Sight Word Catcher

Cut and fold the Fun Flap.

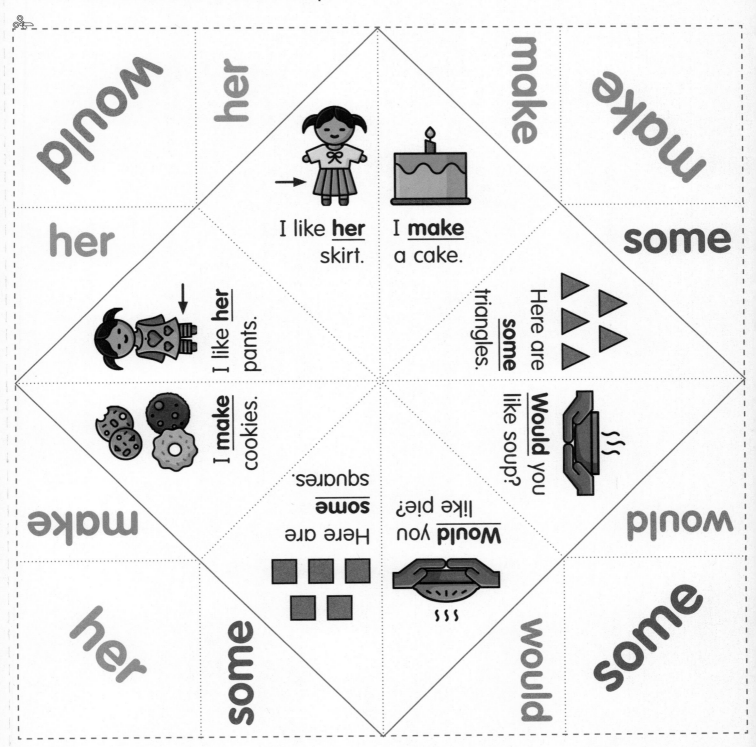

Words to Know

Grown-up: Say the words aloud in a normal voice. Then invite your child to say the words in a silly voice.

into   him

like   time

Say them in a shark voice!

Word Practice

Trace.

like like

like like

I **like** to swim.

Write.

Find each **like**. Color that pumpkin **orange**. Then color the rest of the picture.

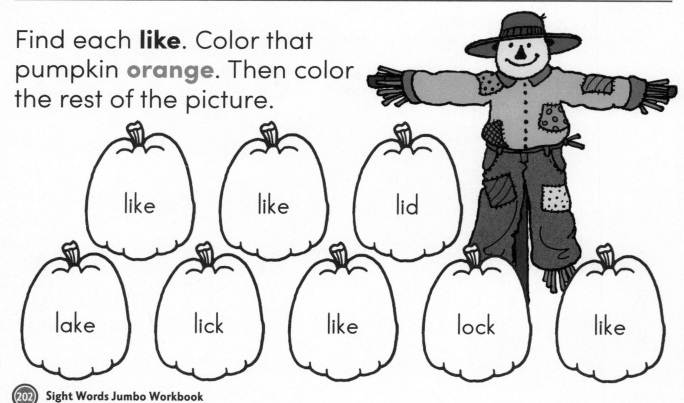

like   like   lid

lake   lick   like   lock   like

Word Practice

Trace.

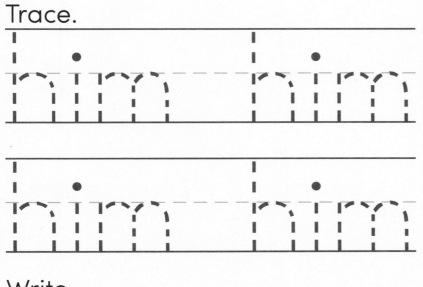

him   him

nim   nim

The ball came back to **him**.

Write.

Circle each **him**. (Hint: There are 6.)

n	j	n	t	a	k	z	u	f	s
h	i	m	g	h	e	d	c	l	o
d	a	l	h	i	w	q	h	i	m
n	h	r	i	m	o	v	b	y	x
w	i	f	m	j	h	i	m	t	k
b	m	u	q	c	s	e	g	p	r

Scholastic Inc.

Word Practice

Trace.

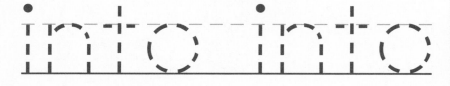

He jumped **into** the pool.

Write.

Find each **into**. Color that train car **blue**.
Then color the rest of the picture.

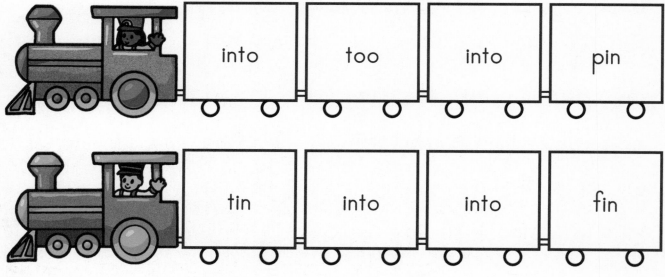

into   too   into   pin

tin   into   into   fin

Word Practice

Trace.

It is **time** to wake up!

Write.

Help the rabbit get to the tea party.
Color the clocks with **time**.

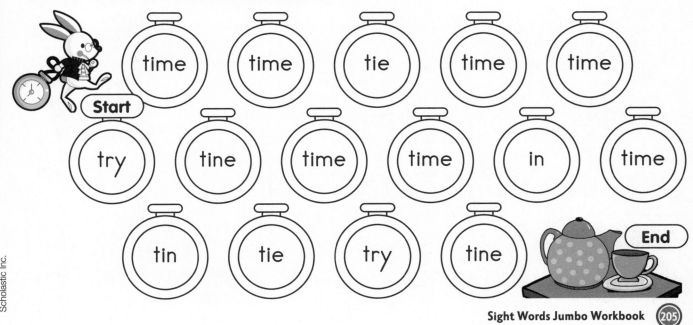

What's Missing?

Fill in the boxes to make words from the list.

1. h ☐ m

2. t i ☐ e

3. ☐ n t o

4. l i k ☐

o Word List
   like
o him
   into
o time

~~~~~~~~~~~~~~~~~~~~~~~~~~~~~~~~~~~~~~

Complete the sentences. Use the word list.

1. The students walk _____ school.

2. Puppies _____ to play.

3. Watch _____ throw.

4. It is _____ to go to the park.

Scholastic Inc.

Sight Word Sentences

Write the sight word to complete the sentences.
Read the sentences aloud.

I _____ to read.

I _____ to play.

I _____ to draw.

I _____ to sing.

I _____ to laugh.

like

Scholastic Inc.

Word Sort

Cut out the bats on page 209. Sort them into the caves.

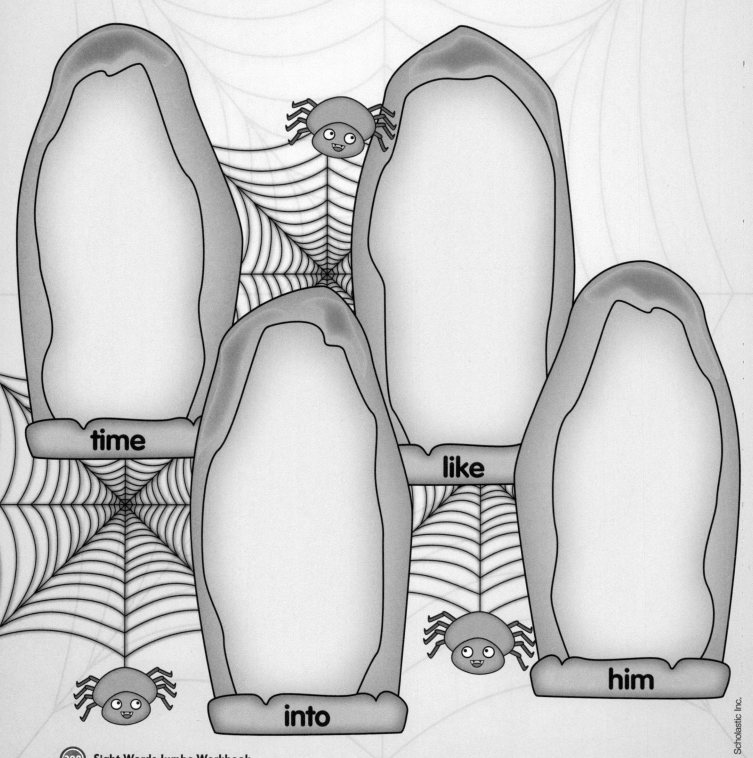

time

like

into

him

Sight Word Catcher

Cut and fold the Fun Flap.

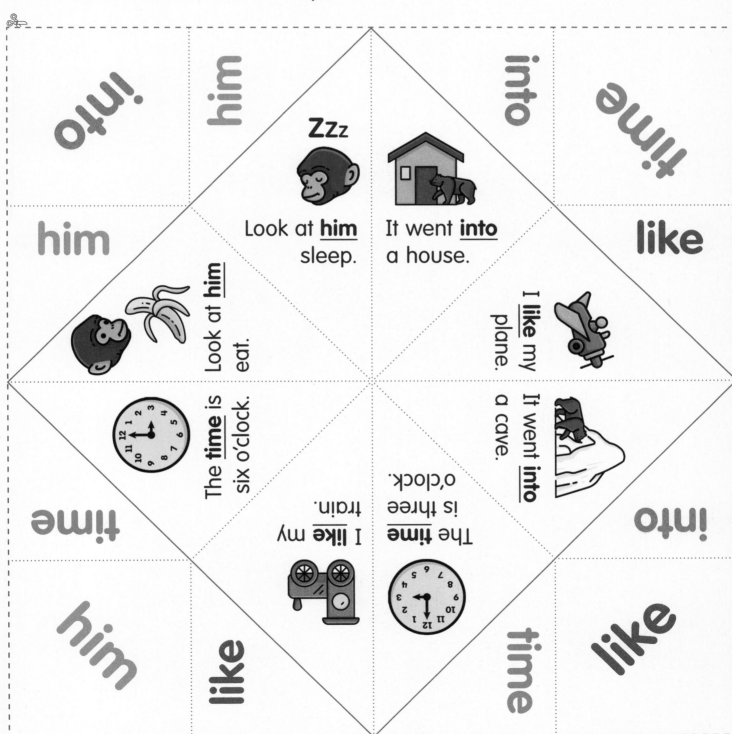

Words to Know

Grown-up: Say the words aloud in a normal voice. Then invite your child to say the words in a silly voice.

two

look

has

more

Say them in a **weightlifter** voice!

Word Practice

Trace.

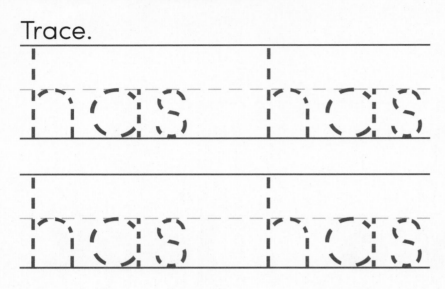

It **has**
a hat.

Write.

Find each **has**. Color that space yellow. Then color the rest of the picture.

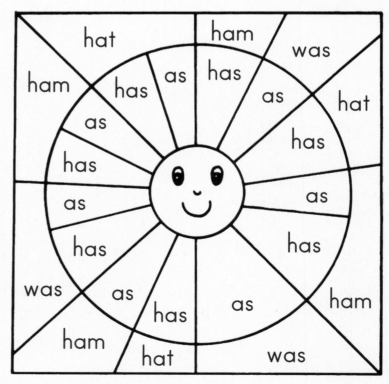

Scholastic Inc.

Word Practice

Trace.

Come **look**
at the clown.

Write.

Circle each **look**. (Hint: There are 6.)

t	a	l	o	o	k	n	y	h	l
l	f	u	d	c	b	e	s	m	o
o	g	q	l	a	l	o	o	k	o
o	r	x	o	n	p	c	f	u	k
k	i	h	o	r	v	w	n	g	j
f	m	b	k	z	l	o	o	k	e

Scholastic Inc.

Word Practice

Trace.

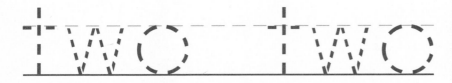

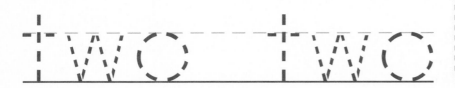

I have **two** eyes.

Write.

Circle the key rings with **two** keys.

Word Practice

Trace.

Do you want some **more**?

Write.

In each set, circle the group that has **more**.

 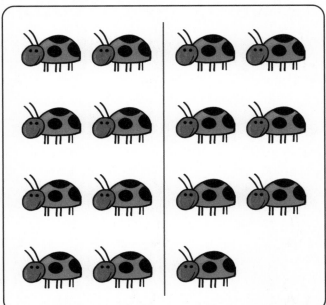

What's Missing?

Fill in the boxes to make words from the list.

1. l ☐ o k

2. h a ☐

3. m o ☐ e

4. t ☐ o

Word List
has
look
two
more

Complete the sentences. Use the word list.

1. I see _____ birds.

2. Chris needs _____ glue.

3. My neighbor _____ dogs.

4. Come _____ at the computer.

Scholastic Inc.

Tic-Tac Sight Word

Play the games below. The word with three Xs or Os wins!

Place an **X** over **has**.
(Circle) **look**.

has	look	look
has	look	has
has	has	look

This word won: _____

Place an **X** over **two**.
(Circle) **more**.

two	more	more
two	two	more
more	two	two

This word won: _____

Place an **X** over **has**.
(Circle) **more**.

has	has	more
more	has	more
has	more	more

This word won: _____

Place an **X** over **two**.
(Circle) **look**.

two	look	two
look	look	two
two	look	look

This word won: _____

Scholastic Inc.

Word Sort

Cut out the pumpkins on page 221.
Sort them onto the vines.

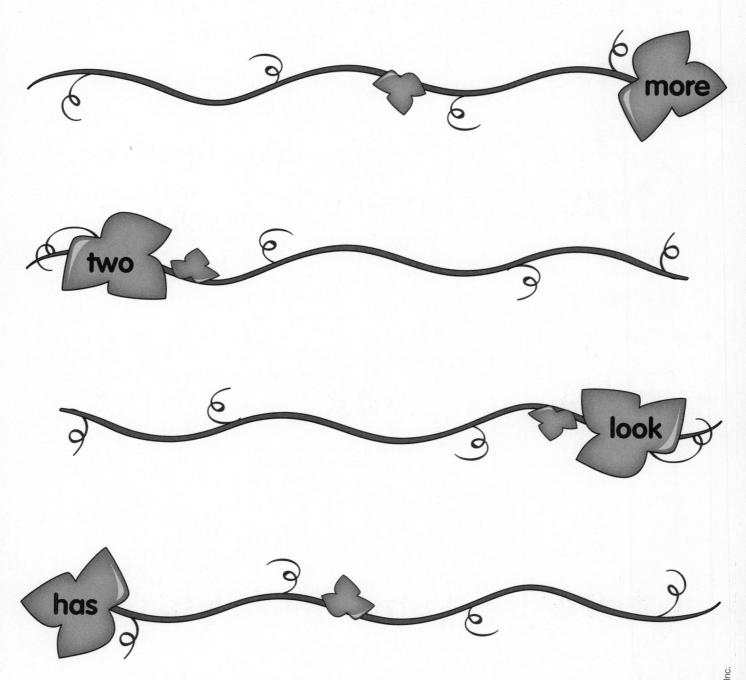

Scholastic Inc.

Sight Word Catcher

Cut and fold the Fun Flap.

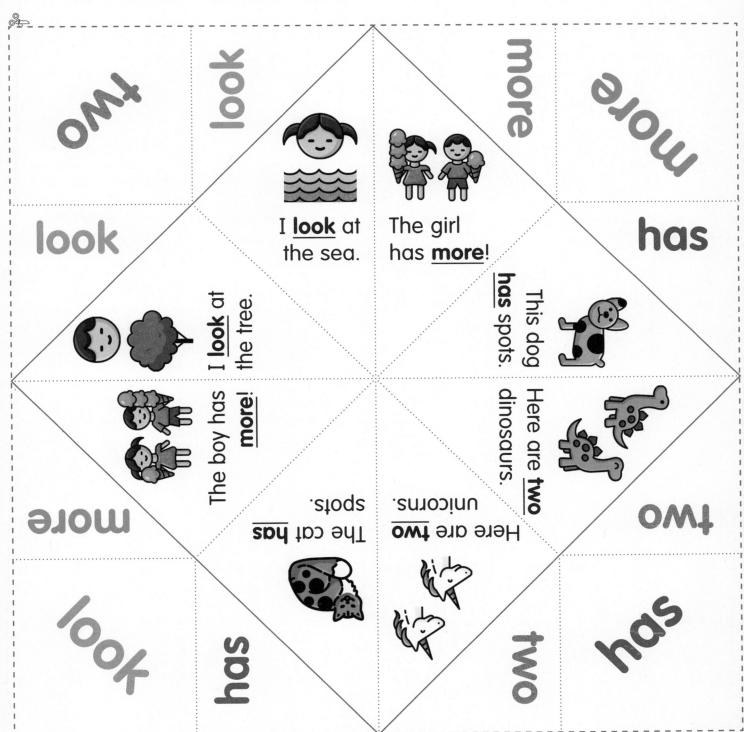

Words to Know

Grown-up: Say the words aloud in a normal voice. Then invite your child to say the words in a silly voice.

number

see

go

write

Say them in a snake voice!

Word Practice

Trace.

Write.

I will **write** a letter.

Find each **write**. Color that space **orange**. Then color the rest of the picture.

Scholastic Inc.

Word Practice

Trace.

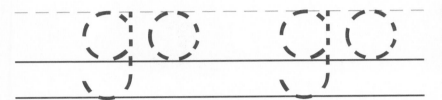

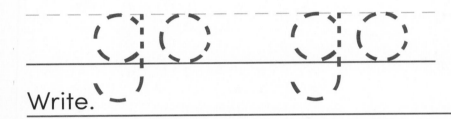

A train can **go** fast!

Write.

Circle each **go**. (Hint: There are 6.)

q e h g c z n a l f

g o v o j g u r m d

u n p k f o b i t j

x r g a d y e v c s

y l o q s t w g o x

f i b m g o h p z k

Word Practice

Trace.

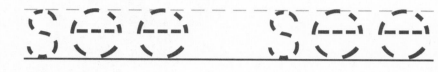

Can you **see** what the bear has?

Write.

Find each **see**. Color that space yellow. Then color the rest of the picture.

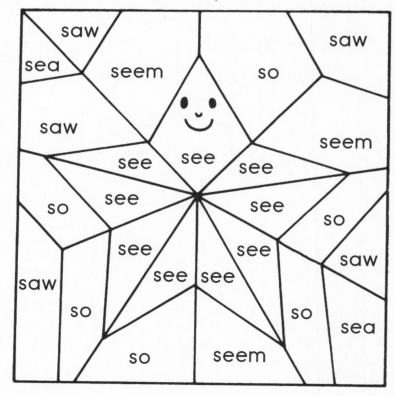

Word Practice

Trace.

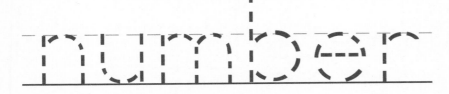

My favorite **number** is 6.

Write.

Find each **number**. Color that cup **pink**.
Then color the rest of the picture.

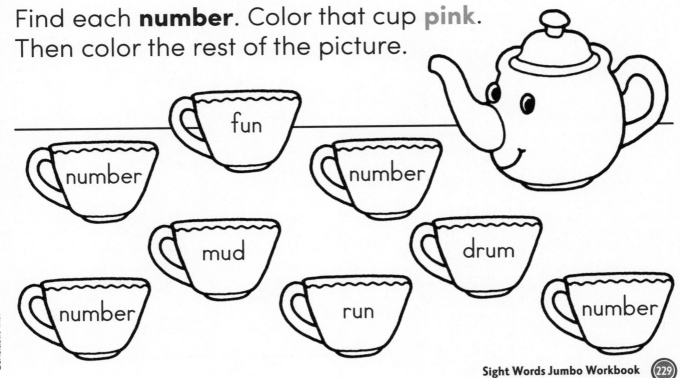

What's Missing?

Fill in the boxes to make words from the list.

Word List
write
go
see
number

1. ☐ e e

2. w r ☐ t e

3. g ☐

4. n ☐ m b e r

Complete the sentences. Use the word list.

1. I _____ to bed at 8:00 p.m.

2. Use a pencil to _____ your name.

3. Do you _____ the bird?

4. I am her _____ one fan.

Sight Word Sentences

Write the sight word to complete the sentences.
Read the sentences aloud.

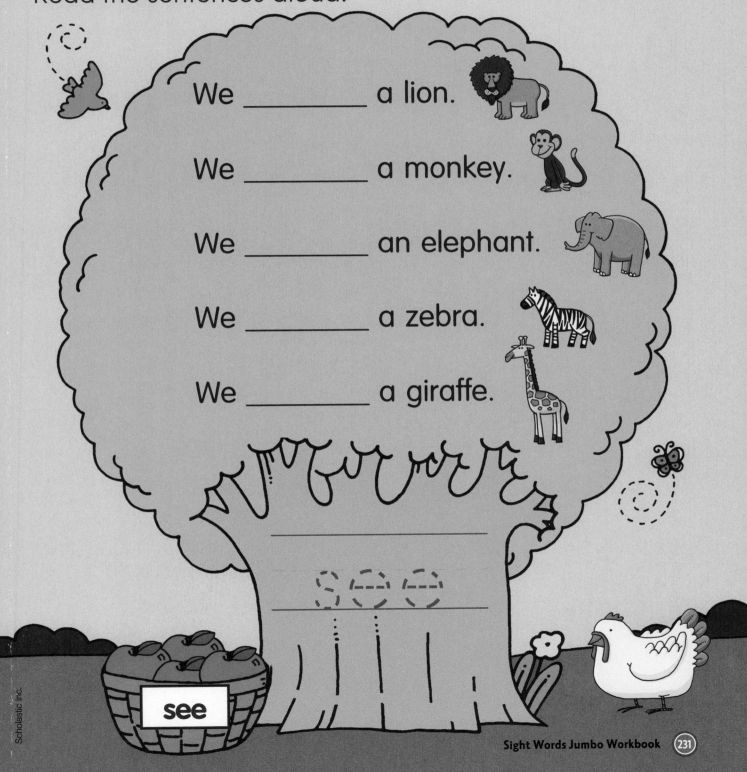

We _____ a lion.

We _____ a monkey.

We _____ an elephant.

We _____ a zebra.

We _____ a giraffe.

see

see

Scholastic Inc.

Word Sort

Cut out the chicks on page 233.
Sort them under the hens.

number   see   write   go

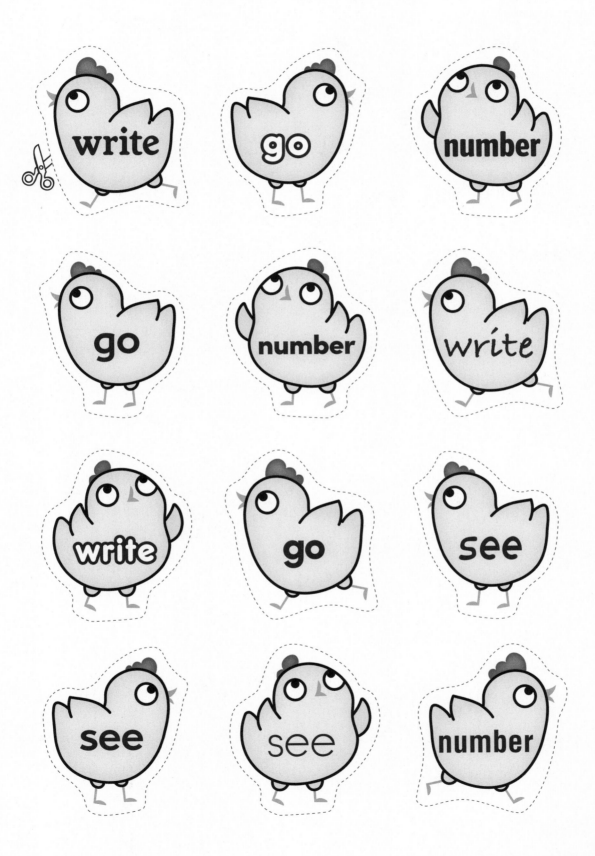

Sight Word Catcher

Cut and fold the Fun Flap.

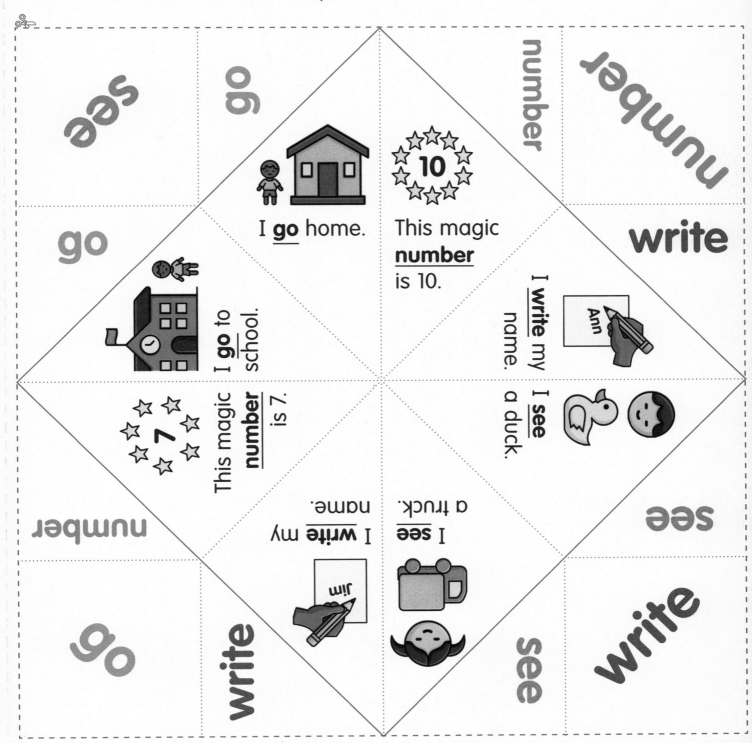

Words to Know

Grown-up: Say the words aloud in a normal voice. Then invite your child to say the words in a silly voice.

could people

no way

Say them in a game show announcer voice!

Word Practice

Trace.

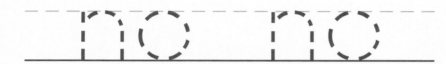

No, thanks. I'm full.

Write.

Find each **no**. Color that space **green**. Then color the rest of the picture.

Scholastic Inc.

Word Practice

Trace.

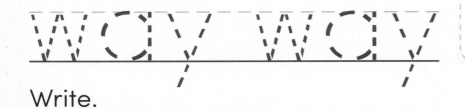

Write.

It is **way** up there.

Find each **way**. Color that bee yellow.
Then color the rest of the picture.

Scholastic Inc.

Word Practice

Trace.

He **could** ride all day!

Write.

Circle each **could**. (Hint: There are 6.)

p c n c o u l d h c
e o s t b r x c f o
g u c o u l d o j u
a l x h z p m u e l
y d k v a n w l t d
c o u l d i q d r s

Word Practice

Trace.

people

people

The **people** are sleeping.

Write.

Find each **people**. Color that space **red**.
Then color the rest of the picture.

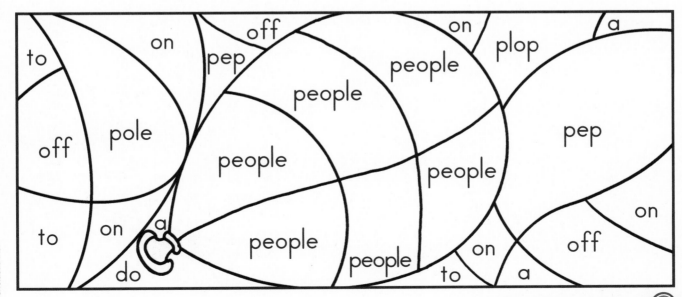

What's Missing?

Fill in the boxes to make words from the list.

Word List
no
way
could
people

1. c o u ☐ d

2. n ☐

3. ☐ a y

4. p ☐ o p l e

Complete the sentences. Use the word list.

1. The _____ are jumping.

2. I have paper but _____ pencil.

3. She knows the _____ to the zoo.

4. I wish I _____ come to your party.

Scholastic Inc.

Sight Word Maze

Help the mouse find the strawberry basket.
Find the path with the word **could**.

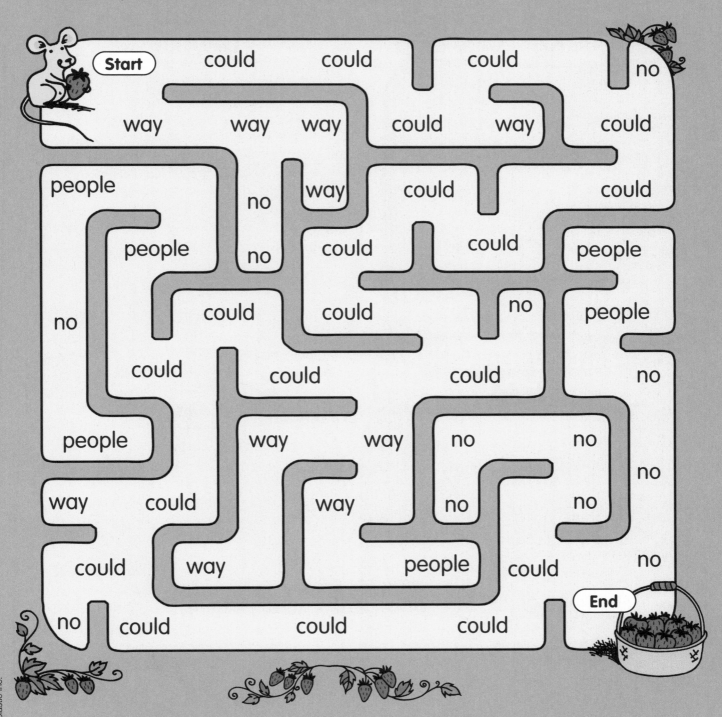

Word Sort

Cut out the cookies on page 245. Sort them into the jars.

Sight Words Jumbo Workbook

Scholastic Inc.

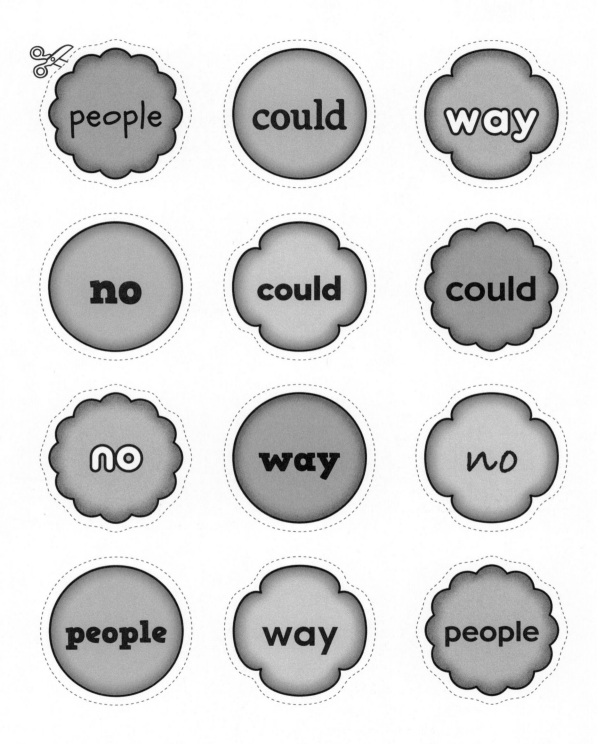

Sight Word Catcher

Cut and fold the Fun Flap.

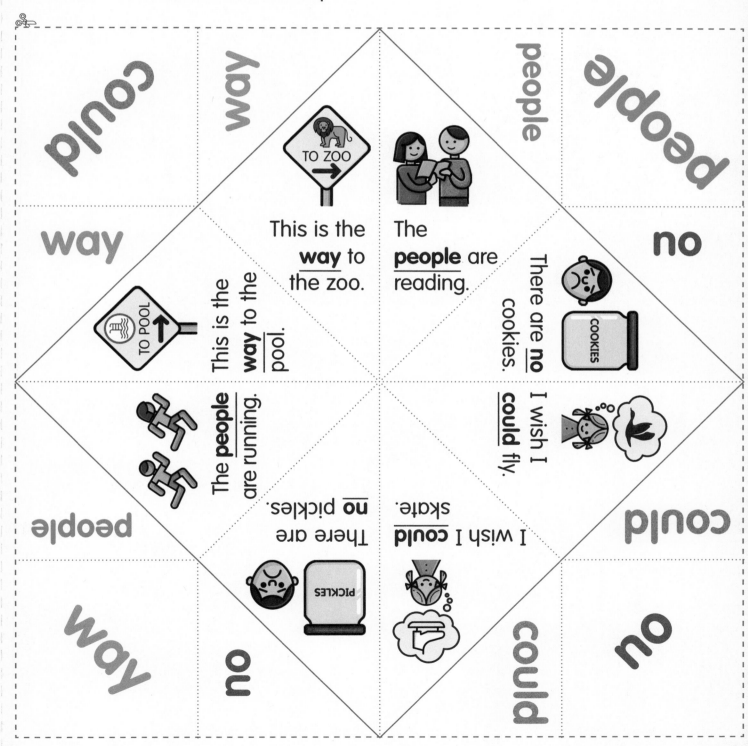

Words to Know

Grown-up: Say the words aloud in a normal voice. Then invite your child to say the words in a silly voice.

first

water

my

than

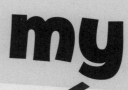

Say them in a lion voice!

Word Practice

Trace.

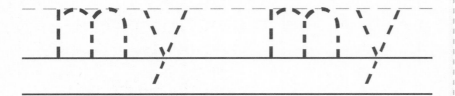

This is **my** cat.

Write.

Find each **my**. Color that space **green**. Then color the rest of the picture.

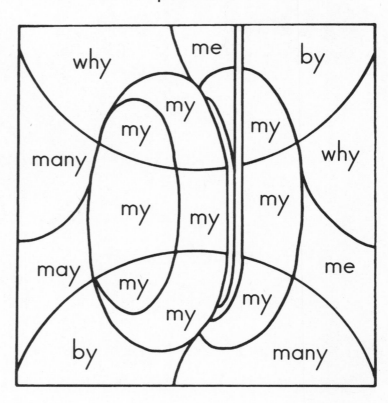

Scholastic Inc.

Word Practice

Trace.

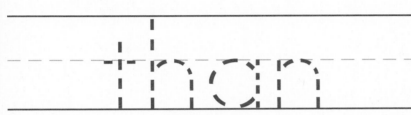

I like dogs
more **than** cats.

Write.

Circle each **than**. (Hint: There are 6.)

q   t   h   a   n   h   a   n   a   n   a   t
g   t   t   v   t   h   a   n   m   h
t   h   h   k   t   e   r   j   t   a
h   e   a   a   h   q   v   h   s   n
a   r   n   t   a   a   n   e   k   g
n   l   o   j   n   b   p   r   c   f

Scholastic Inc.

Word Practice

Trace.

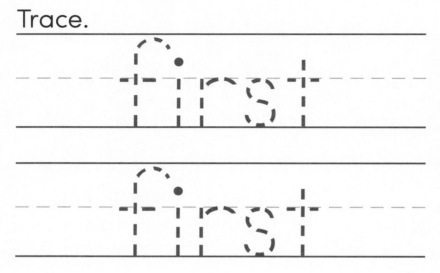

I lost my
first tooth!

Write.

Find each **first**. Color that space **orange**.
Then color the rest of the picture.

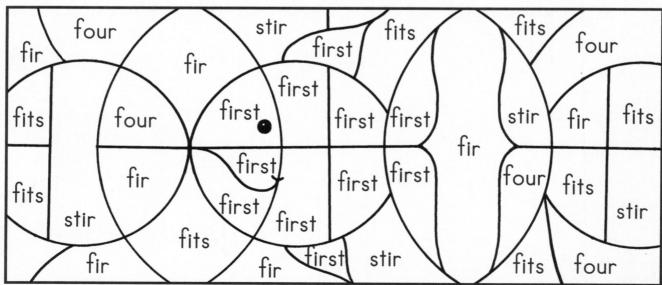

Scholastic Inc.

Word Practice

Trace.

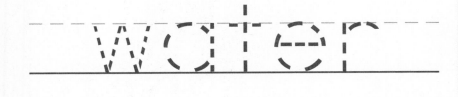

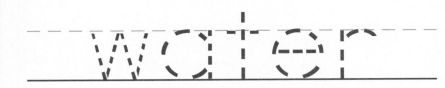

This **water** is warm!

Write.

Find each **water**. Color that flag **blue**. Then color the rest of the picture.

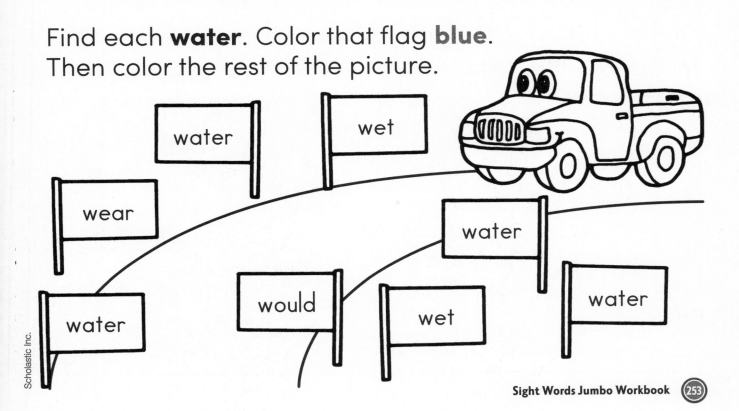

water

wet

wear

water

water

would

wet

water

What's Missing?

Fill in the boxes to make words from the list.

o Word List
my
o than
first
o water

1. f i ☐ s t

2. m ☐

3. w a ☐ e r

4. t ☐ a n

Complete the sentences. Use the word list.

1. I drank the _____.

2. I gave _____ bike to her.

3. I like red more _____ blue.

4. The _____ person to finish wins!

Tic-Tac Sight Word

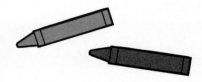

Play the games below. The word with three Xs or Os wins!

Place an **X** over **my**.
(Circle) **than**.

my	my	than
my	than	than
than	my	my

This word won: _____

Place an **X** over **first**.
(Circle) **water**.

first	water	first
water	water	water
first	first	water

This word won: _____

Place an **X** over **my**.
(Circle) **water**.

water	my	water
my	my	my
my	water	water

This word won: _____

Place an **X** over **first**.
(Circle) **than**.

first	than	than
first	first	than
than	than	first

This word won: _____

Scholastic Inc.

Review: my, than, first, water

Sight Word Maze

Help the turtle get to its friend. Connect a path by coloring each log with a list word.

Word List

my	first
than	water

Start

 water
 me
 other

then
first
many
their

their
than
my
my

me
time
look
first

look
two
then
than

make
number
the
water

for
many
many

 **End**

256 **Sight Words Jumbo Workbook**

Scholastic Inc.

Sight Word Catcher

Cut and fold the Fun Flap.

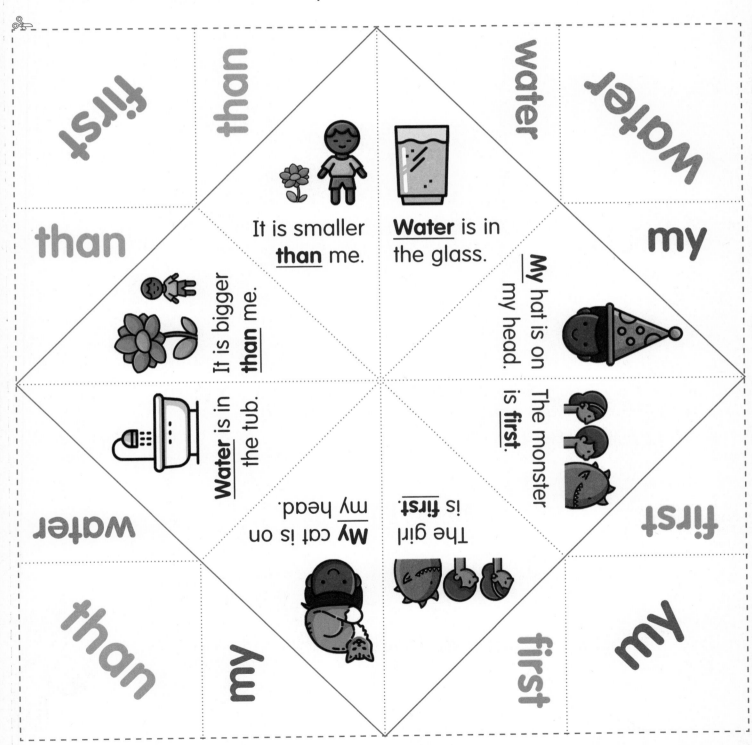

Words to Know

Grown-up: Say the words aloud in a normal voice. Then invite your child to say the words in a silly voice.

been **who**

am **called**

Say them in a surfer voice!

Word Practice

Trace.

been

been

He has **been** in the bath.

Write.

Find each **been**.
Color that space **purple**.
Then color the rest
of the picture.

Scholastic Inc.

Word Practice

Trace.

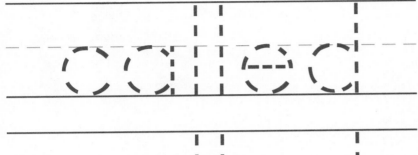

Write.

He is
called Elvis.

Find each **called**.
Color that space **pink**.
Then color the rest
of the picture.

called

called

called

called

call

call

called

called

call

came

came

Scholastic Inc.

Word Practice

Trace.

who who

who who

Who wants to play?

Write.

Find each **who**. Color that bag **red**.
Then color the rest of the picture.

who

was

who

why

we

who

well

who

Scholastic Inc.

Word Practice

Trace.

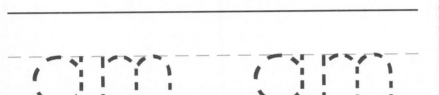

I **am** making a snack.

Write.

Circle each **am**. (Hint: There are 6.)

g	l	u	d	y	q	n	k	v	a
a	z	b	r	e	s	p	i	t	m
m	o	x	a	m	w	v	j	h	b
v	k	h	f	u	t	a	g	c	l
s	j	p	i	c	o	m	r	a	m
q	w	a	m	z	d	y	e	n	f

What's Missing?

Fill in the boxes to make words from the list.

Word List
been
called
who
am

1. w h ☐

2. c ☐ l l e d

3. b e e ☐

4. ☐ m

Complete the sentences. Use the word list.

1. He _____ his aunt on the phone.

2. I _____ six years old.

3. Have you _____ to the library?

4. Sue is _____ I saw yesterday.

Sight Word Maze

Help the boy catch the fish.
Find the path with the word **who**.

Start

been	am	who		who	am	called	called
called	called	been	am	who	am	am	am
called	am	am	am		am	am	am	am
		who						
am	am	am	called		am	been	called
am	been	been	who	who		called	am
					been		
been	been	am	called			called
been	called	who	called	been	am	am
been	who		am	am	am	been	been
been	am	am	called	called

End

Scholastic Inc.

Word Sort

Cut out the puppies on page 267.
Sort them under the dogs.

am

been

who

called

Sight Word Catcher

Cut and fold the Fun Flap.

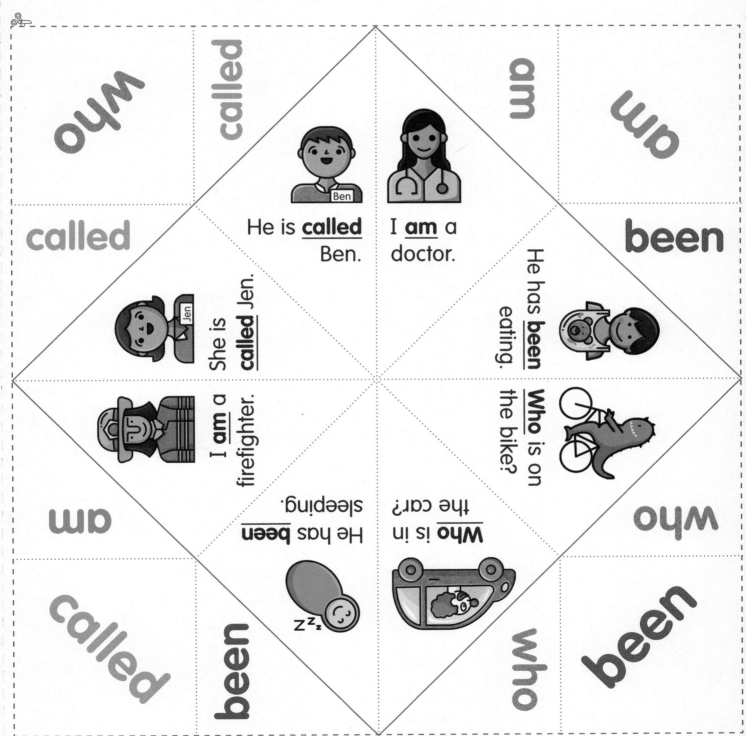

Words to Know

Grown-up: Say the words aloud in a normal voice. Then invite your child to say the words in a silly voice.

find long

its now

Say them in a **dragon** voice!

Word Practice

Trace.

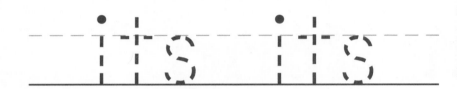

Look at **its** antlers.

Write.

Find each **its**. Color that book **blue**.
Then color the rest of the picture.

it

its

bits

its

it

its

wits

its

Word Practice

Trace.

We have to leave **now**.

Write.

Find each **now**. Color that space yellow. Then color the rest of the picture.

Scholastic Inc.

Word Practice

Trace.

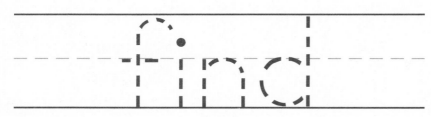

Let's **find** out
if it flies!

Write.

Circle each **find**. (Hint: There are 6.)

f	i	n	d	o	z	p	y	f	f
g	t	u	v	c	f	i	n	d	i
n	f	s	f	h	e	r	j	n	n
f	i	x	i	m	q	v	h	d	d
y	n	w	n	i	f	i	n	d	g
t	d	o	d	d	b	p	r	c	f

Word Practice

Trace.

long

long

How **long**
is the snake?

Write.

Find each **long**. Color that acorn **brown**.
Then color the rest of the picture.

long

kick

lick

long

like

long

long

lock

What's Missing?

Fill in the boxes to make words from the list.

1. f i ☐ d

2. ☐ o w

3. i t ☐

4. l ☐ n g

○ Word List

its

○ now

find

○ long

Complete the sentences. Use the word list.

1. I want to play _____!

2. I pet _____ fur.

3. Did you _____ the book?

4. Her hair is _____.

Word Search

Circle the words from the word list. The words go across and down. The words appear more than once.

Word Bank

its	now	find	long

```
n  o  w  f  e  n  x  n  o  w  l  i
o  f  p  y  i  t  s  o  f  d  o  t
u  l  o  n  g  e  j  u  i  r  n  s
f  i  n  d  l  o  n  g  n  b  g  f
n  i  t  s  f  n  o  w  d  s  u  i
o  f  f  i  n  d  i  l  e  n  x  n
w  i  p  n  l  u  t  o  l  n  l  f
i  n  n  o  o  e  s  s  o  n  o  i
t  d  o  w  n  l  o  n  g  o  n  n
s  i  t  s  g  f  i  n  d  w  g  d
```

Word Sort

Cut out the ice cream scoops on page 279.
Sort them onto the cones or cups.

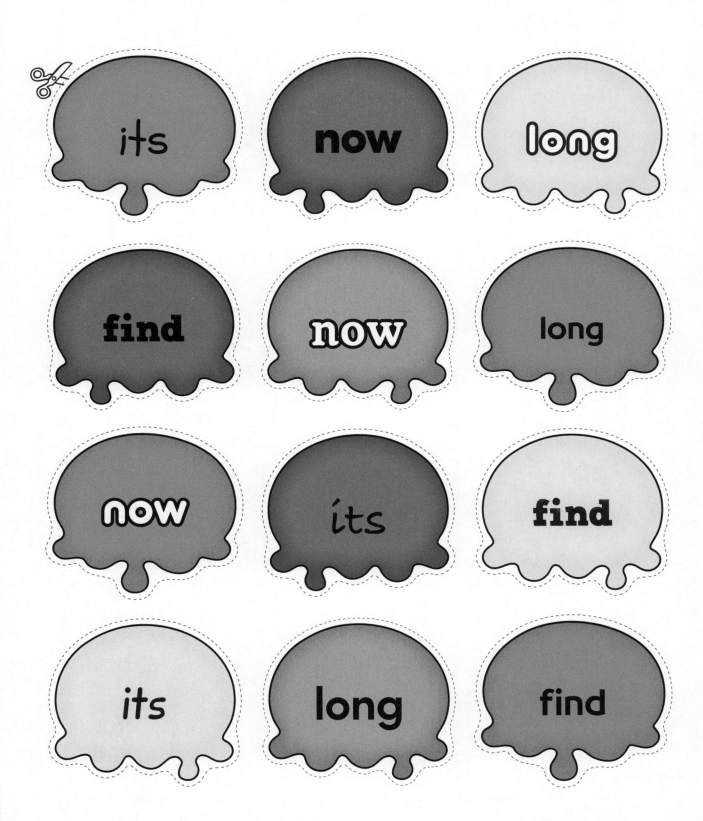

Sight Word Catcher

Cut and fold the Fun Flap.

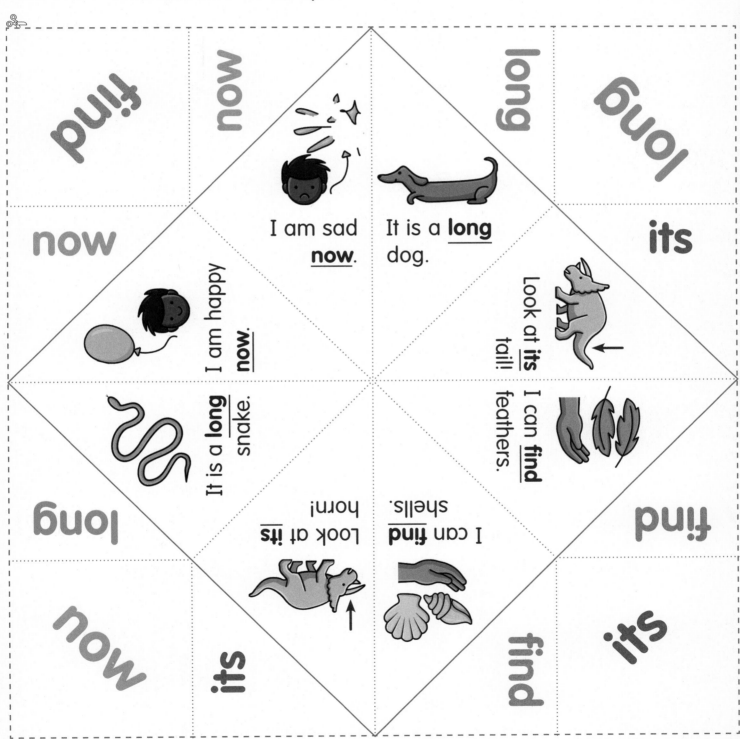

Words to Know

Grown-up: Say the words aloud in a normal voice. Then invite your child to say the words in a silly voice.

did

day

down

get

Say them in a scarecrow voice!

Word Practice

Trace.

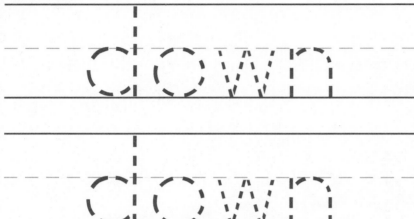

Write.

Our ball went **down** the hill.

Circle each **down**. (Hint: There are 6.)

i	d	o	w	n	b	u	m	r	d
d	c	e	d	o	w	n	q	h	o
o	t	a	v	s	g	d	x	p	w
w	d	o	w	n	z	o	f	c	n
n	l	h	u	m	e	w	s	g	k
f	p	r	j	y	i	n	b	a	v

Word Practice

Trace.

I brush my teeth two times a **day**.

Write.

Circle the items you see during the **day**.

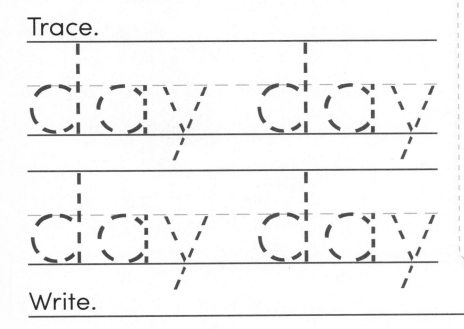

Scholastic Inc.

Word Practice

Trace.

did did

did did

Where **did** the squirrel go?

Write.

Circle each **did**. (Hint: There are 6.)

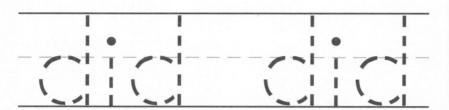

d	a	p	f	o	n	d	i	d	v
i	h	u	d	g	b	v	l	m	q
d	s	c	i	k	d	r	d	i	d
t	m	x	d	e	i	p	f	g	b
y	l	r	n	h	d	w	o	c	k
f	d	i	d	t	z	j	y	e	f

Word Practice

Trace.

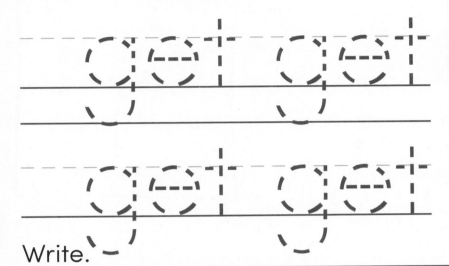

Write.

Could you **get** me the truck?

Find each **get**. Color that ribbon **blue**.
Then color the rest of the picture.

What's Missing?

Fill in the boxes to make words from the list.

Word List
down
day
did
get

1. d a ☐

2. g ☐ t

3. ☐ i d

4. d ☐ w n

Complete the sentences. Use the word list.

1. It rained all _____.

2. Where _____ she go?

3. She will _____ a puppy.

4. He fell _____.

Scholastic Inc.

Sight Word Maze

Help the hamster find its friend.
Find the path with the word **down**.

Sight Word Sentences

Write the sight word to complete the sentences.
Read the sentences aloud.

Go _____ the hill.

Go _____ the slide.

Go _____ the stairs.

Go _____ the ladder.

Go _____ the road.

down

Scholastic Inc.

Sight Word Catcher

Cut and fold the Fun Flap.

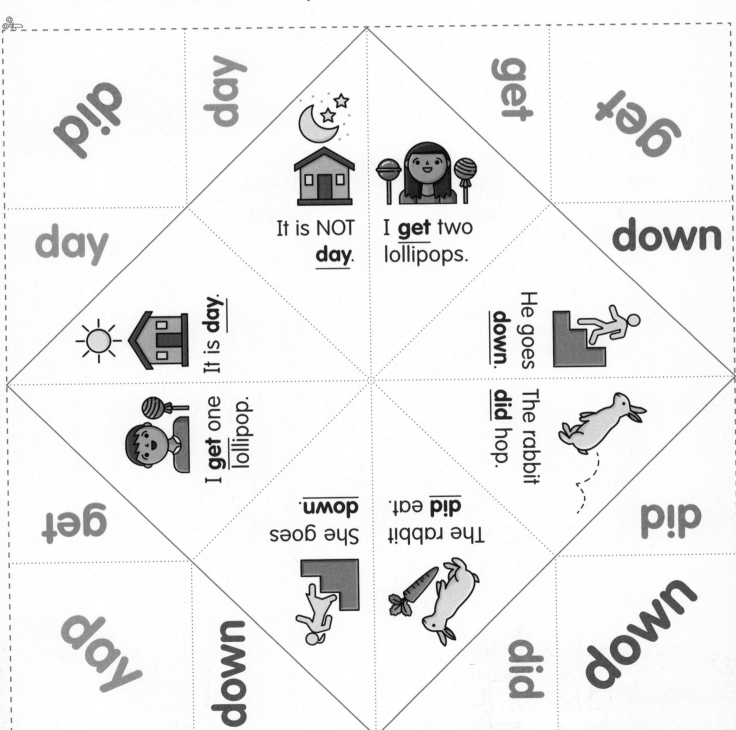

did

day

get

get

day

It is NOT **day**.

I **get** two lollipops.

down

It is **day**.

I **get** one lollipop.

He goes **down**.

The rabbit **did** hop.

get

The rabbit **did** eat.

She goes **down**.

did

day

down

did

down

Words to Know

Grown-up: Say the words aloud in a normal voice. Then invite your child to say the words in a silly voice.

may

made

come

part

Say them in a gnome voice!

Word Practice

Trace.

come

come

Write.

Come here!

Find each **come**. Color that space **orange**.
Then color the rest of the picture.

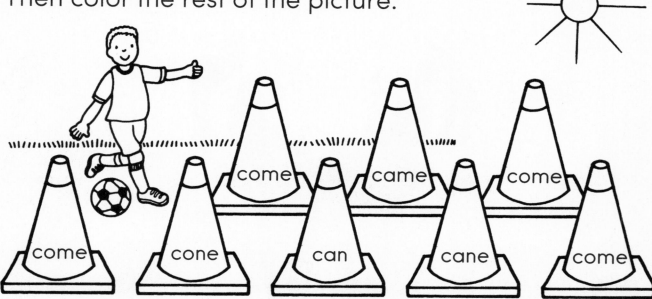

come   cone   come   came   come

come   cone   can   cane   come

Scholastic Inc.

Word Practice

Trace.

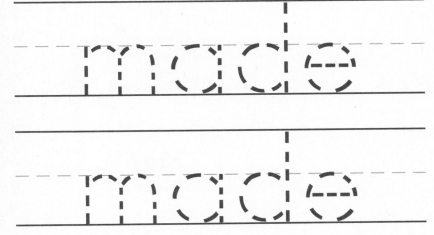

Write.

I **made** it!

Circle each **made**. (Hint: There are 6.)

p	c	n	m	o	u	m	a	d	e
e	o	s	a	m	a	d	e	f	o
m	u	c	d	u	l	d	o	j	m
a	l	x	e	z	p	m	u	e	a
d	d	m	a	d	e	w	l	t	d
e	o	u	l	d	i	q	d	r	e

Word Practice

Trace.

may

may

May I ask a question?

Write.

Help the rabbit get a snack. Color the carrots with **may**.

Scholastic Inc.

Word Practice

Trace.

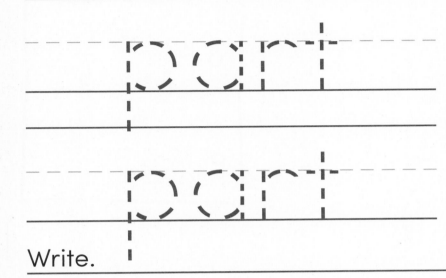

Write.

This **part**
is the petal.

Find each **part**.
Color that space
orange. Then color
the rest of the
picture.

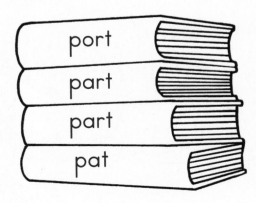

port
part
part
pat

pat
part
art
part
part
port
pan
part

Scholastic Inc.

What's Missing?

Fill in the boxes to make words from the list.

Word List
come
made
may
part

1. m a ☐

2. p ☐ r t

3. ☐ a d e

4. c o ☐ e

Complete the sentences. Use the word list.

1. He is _____ of Ms. Chu's class.

2. I _____ a new friend.

3. Nina _____ have dessert.

4. What time will you _____ over?

Tic-Tac Sight Word

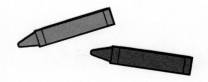

Play the games below. The word with three Xs or Os wins!

Place an **X** over **come**.
(Circle) **made**.

come	made	come
made	come	made
come	made	made

This word won: _____

Place an **X** over **may**.
(Circle) **part**.

part	may	part
part	may	may
may	may	part

This word won: _____

Place an **X** over **come**.
(Circle) **part**.

part	come	part
come	part	part
part	come	come

This word won: _____

Place an **X** over **may**.
(Circle) **made**.

made	made	made
may	may	made
made	may	may

This word won: _____

Scholastic Inc.

Word Sort

Cut out the beach balls on page 301.
Sort them onto the beach blankets.

come

made

may

part

come made may

part may made

come made may

part come part

Sight Word Catcher

Cut and fold the Fun Flap.

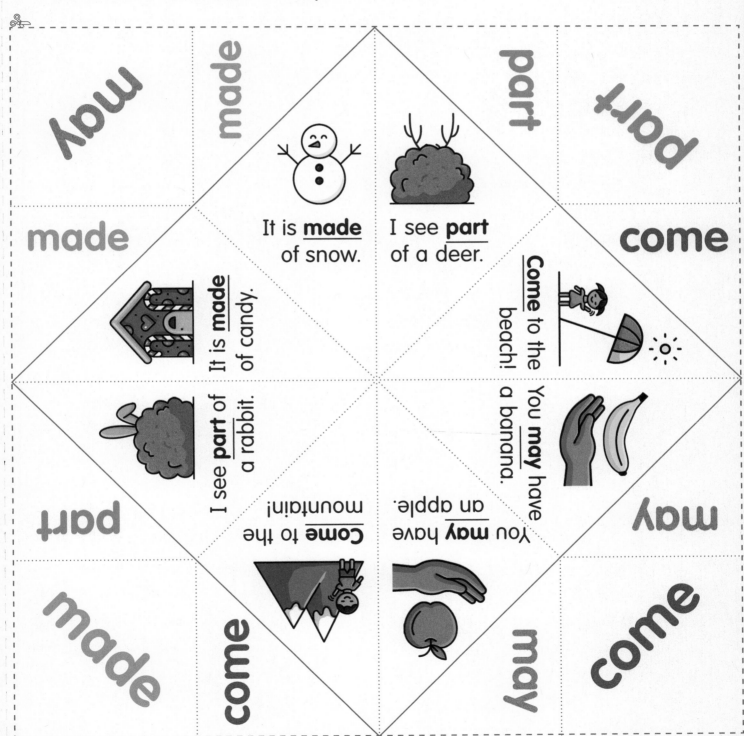

Making and Using the Flash Cards

MAKING THE FLASH CARDS

Remove pages 307–318 along the perforations. Then carefully cut apart the sight word cards. To keep the cards tidy, store them in a plastic zip-close bag or a shoebox decorated with— you guessed it!—sight words.

FUN FLASH CARD ACTIVITIES

Reinforce your child's sight word knowledge with these easy activities. Then tap his/her imagination to make up some new games!

1. **GO FISH:** Place some or all of the flash cards in a paper bag. Invite your child to pick a card at random, then read both sides aloud. If the card is read correctly, he or she keeps it. When 10 cards are collected, your child wins.

2. **SILLY SENTENCES:** Ask your child to pick three flash cards at random, challenging him or her to say or write a sentence that contains all three sight words. Repeat with new cards.

3. **SIGHT WORD SEEK-AND-WRITE:** Place 10 or more flash cards around a room, and set a timer for two minutes. Can your child find and read all 10 sight words before the timer goes off?

4. **FILL-IN-THE-BLANKS:** There are several blank cards included in this set. Look up the next 100 words on the Fry Sight Words list, add some to the cards, and continue the sight word learning!

SIGHT WORD CHECK-IN

For a quick assessment of your child's sight word mastery, use the Sight Word List on page 10. Here's how: Shuffle the flash cards, and hold up random sight words for your child to read. When a word is read correctly, put a ✓ on the sheet. When a word is not read correctly, circle the word. If you find that your child is struggling with certain sight words, reteach them via these flash cards and/or activities.

the	in
of	is
and	you
a	that
to	it

he	as
was	with
for	his
on	they
are	I

at	or
be	one
this	had
have	by
from	words

but	we
not	when
what	your
all	can
were	said

there	she
use	do
an	how
each	their
which	if

will	many
up	then
other	them
about	these
out	so

some	him
her	into
would	time
make	has
like	look

two	number
more	no
write	way
go	could
see	people

my	called
than	who
first	am
water	its
been	now

find	get
long	come
down	made
day	may
did	part

Scholastic Inc.

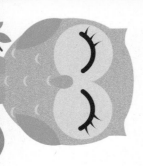

Sight Words Jumbo

SCHOLASTIC

You're a Scholastic Superstar!

has completed the
Scholastic Sight Words
Jumbo Workbook.

Presented on
_____

Congratulations!